NEW DIRECTIONS FOR CHILD DEVELOPMENT

William Damon, *Brown University*
EDITOR-IN-CHIEF

Academic Instruction in Early Childhood: Challenge or Pressure?

Leslie Rescorla
Bryn Mawr College

Marion C. Hyson
University of Delaware

Kathy Hirsh-Pasek
Temple University

EDITORS

Number 53, Fall 1991

JOSSEY-BASS INC., PUBLISHERS, San Francisco

MAXWELL MACMILLAN INTERNATIONAL PUBLISHING GROUP
New York • Oxford • Singapore • Sydney • Toronto

ACADEMIC INSTRUCTION IN EARLY CHILDHOOD: CHALLENGE OR PRESSURE?
Leslie Rescorla, Marion C. Hyson, Kathy Hirsh-Pasek (eds.)
New Directions for Child Development, no. 53
William Damon, Editor-in-Chief

Microfilm copies of issues and articles are available in 16mm and 35mm,
as well as microfiche in 105mm, through University Microfilms Inc., 300
North Zeeb Road, Ann Arbor, Michigan 48106.

LC 85-644581   ISSN 0195-2269   ISBN 1-55542-769-3

NEW DIRECTIONS FOR CHILD DEVELOPMENT is part of The Jossey-Bass
Education Series and is published quarterly by Jossey-Bass Inc., Publishers, 350 Sansome Street, San Francisco, California 94104-1310 (publication number USPS 494-090). Second-class postage paid at San Francisco,
California, and at additional mailing offices. POSTMASTER: Send address
changes to Jossey-Bass Inc., Publishers, 350 Sansome Street, San Francisco, California 94104.

SUBSCRIPTIONS for 1991 cost $48.00 for individuals and $70.00 for institutions, agencies, and libraries.

EDITORIAL CORRESPONDENCE should be sent to the Editor-in-Chief,
William Damon, Department of Education, Box 1938, Brown University,
Providence, Rhode Island 02912.

Cover photograph by Wernher Krutein/PHOTOVAULT © 1990.

Printed on acid-free paper in the United States of America.

CONTENTS

Editors' Notes

Parents, educators, and developmental psychologists have been engaged in a heated debate over the costs and benefits of emphasizing academic skills in early childhood. Some have argued that formal academic instruction and high performance expectations give young children a head start on school achievement. Others have held just as strongly that these expectations are developmentally inappropriate, leading only to superficial learning and damaging pressures.

"Hothousing" and "hurrying" are terms that have become identified with affluent parents and status-conscious preschools. However, the issue of early academics is much broader. Concerns about the quality and availability of child care, about the urgent need for early intervention in children's lives, about the adequacy of American education in a changing world, and about parents' involvement in their children's early development have stimulated the establishment of more academically rigorous environments for preschool and kindergarten children. These academic environments have been enthusiastically advocated by some individuals and condemned by others.

The controversy over early academics touches on many central problems in developmental psychology, such as the malleability of early development, the relationship between cognitive and affective domains, the nature of adult involvement in early learning, and the social definition of childhood. This volume, *Academic Instruction in Early Childhood: Challenge or Pressure?*, provides resources for those interested in these issues, whether from the perspective of the researcher or of the practitioner. In the first chapter, Leslie Rescorla provides a historical and conceptual introduction to the issues. The following four chapters draw on findings from a program of research conducted by the editors. The Academic Environments study, sponsored by the Spencer Foundation, examined the nature and developmental consequences of parental and school academic expectations among socioeconomically advantaged families in Pennsylvania and Delaware. One hundred and twenty-five families, whose children attended eleven preschools varying in academic emphasis, participated in the initial phase of the project. Subsamples of children and families took part in other aspects of the project. Ninety children and their mothers participated in videotaped interactions, and fifty-six families participated in a follow-up study at the end of kindergarten. Chapters Two, Three, Four, and Five describe findings from several aspects of this research project, conducted collaboratively at the University of Delaware, Temple University, and Bryn Mawr College. In Chapter Two, Leslie Rescorla discusses research on parents' and teachers' attitudes toward early academic instruction, with particular emphasis on measurement issues and on the comparison of parental and teacher beliefs. In Chapter Three,

New Directions for Child Development, no. 53, Fall 1991 © Jossey-Bass Inc., Publishers

Marion C. Hyson deals with the phenomenon of the "academic preschool." The chapter reviews various approaches that have been used in observing academically oriented educational programs and looks at the question of relationships between teachers' attitudes and their classroom practices. In Chapter Four, Marion C. Hyson returns to parental influences, discussing a number of interrelated pathways through which parents may create a hothousing environment in early childhood. In Chapter Five, Kathy Hirsh-Pasek discusses how variations in parental and school academic emphases influence the academic, creative, and affective development of young children.

The next four chapters broaden the perspective on early academics. In Chapter Six, Deborah Stipek discusses one aspect of an ongoing study that examines the effects of variations in preschool and kindergarten curricula on children's immediate classroom behavior and on their later development. Stipek also describes issues involved in characterizing early education programs, using findings from classroom observations of sixty-two programs in California, with a more socioeconomically diverse sample than that represented in the Academic Environments project. In Chapter Seven, David P. Weikart and Lawrence J. Schweinhart focus on the issue of academic programs for socioeconomically disadvantaged children. The chapter uses data from a long-term follow-up of adolescents who had participated in one of several kinds of early intervention programs, including formal academic programs. In Chapter Eight, Dale C. Farran, Beverly Silveri, and Anne Culp discuss the increase in the number of preschool programs for disadvantaged children within public schools. They address the question of the programs' developmental appropriateness, using data from a two-year study in North Carolina. In Chapter Nine, Edward F. Zigler and Elizabeth Gilman place the issue of early academics within a larger concern: the child care crisis in America. The chapter presents research-based policy recommendations that would move the public schools out of a narrow academic role into a central part of the family support system.

In the final chapter of this volume, Irving E. Sigel takes on the task of integrating the preceding discussions of research, policy, and practice within a developmental framework. He critically discusses the phenomenon of the academic preschool as one of many attempts to influence the trajectory of development. Altogether, we hope that these ten chapters stimulate further study and discussion of the issues surrounding early academics.

Leslie Rescorla
Marion C. Hyson
Kathy Hirsh-Pasek
Editors

Leslie Rescorla is associate professor in the Department of Human Development, Bryn Mawr College, Bryn Mawr, Pennsylvania.

Marion C. Hyson is associate professor in the Department of Individual and Family Studies, University of Delaware, Newark.

Kathy Hirsh-Pasek is associate professor in the Department of Psychology, Temple University, Philadelphia.

Should the teacher-directed, academically oriented preschool be the model for the 1990s?

Early Academics: Introduction to the Debate

Leslie Rescorla

The issue of academic experiences for preschool children has been widely debated in recent years. Some professionals argue that formal academic instruction is an important and valuable enrichment experience for preschool children, enabling them to get an early start on school achievement. Other experts condemn academic instruction for young children, arguing that it deprives preschoolers of the opportunity for self-motivated learning and creates feelings of tension and anxiety.

From a historical perspective, this debate about educational experiences for preschoolers can be seen as a clash between two contrasting views of the child that originated in the eighteenth century, if not earlier. One constellation of attitudes, prototypically associated with Jean-Jacques Rousseau, sees the child as an active constructivist who engages in experimentation and exploration as he or she moves through biologically unfolding developmental stages. The contrasting view, associated with John Locke, characterizes the child's cognitive development as shaped by the environmental experiences and learning opportunities provided by adults. Whereas the former viewpoint would deplore early academic instruction for young children, the latter model would see such instruction as valuable and enriching.

Perhaps the most outspoken contemporary thinker on the dangers of academic "pressure" on young children is David Elkind (1981, 1987a). Elkind (1987b) strongly condemns the downward extension of academic curricula to preschool children. For example, he is critical of the practices of providing formal instruction in reading and math and giving dittoed worksheets to young children. Elkind believes that early academic experiences run counter to the preschool child's natural predisposition to learn by exploration and action. He argues that when adults impose their own learning priorities on preschoolers, they interfere with the young child's self-directed learning, create guilt and anxiety, and stifle intrinsic motivation to explore.

Similar themes are expressed by Sigel (1987), who deplores the pressure and stress that "hothousing" creates for young children. Sigel argues strongly that children need to engage in active, self-directed exploration and learning. He and his colleagues have demonstrated that highly didactic and authoritarian teaching of young children produces negative effects on their IQs, reasoning, and problem-solving abilities, and creates anxiety about achievement (Sigel, 1987).

Although professionals such as Elkind and Sigel decry academic pressure, other advocates and experts encourage parents to enrich their children's early years by cultivating their talents and developing their skills (Doman, 1984; Eastman and Barr, 1985; Engelmann and Engelmann, 1981; Ledson, 1975). Some experts on this side of the debate argue strongly for teaching basic reading skills to infants (Doman, 1984). Others take a less extreme position but still emphasize the importance of preparing preschoolers for school, exposing them to new technologies, and capitalizing on their astounding ability to learn. Advocates cite the benefits of learning a foreign language as a young child, the advantages of acquiring computer literacy in the preschool period, the value of developing the discipline necessary for learning at an early age, and the benefits of learning to read as early as possible.

These issues about early schooling for young children were debated at a 1986 conference attended by professionals in child development and social policy, which culminated in the book *Early Schooling: The National Debate* (Kagan and Zigler, 1987). The closing statement by Kagan and Zigler made a strong plea for "developmentally appropriate" programs for young children, as delineated in a publication from the National Association for the Education of Young Children (NAEYC) (Bredekamp, 1987). Kagan and Zigler (1987, p. 220) condemned highly academic programs in very clear terms: "As pressure mounts for children to become achievers at ever younger ages, early education is shifting to a more didactic emphasis, thus evoking images of academic pressure and expectation, rigid classrooms, and formalized learning methods."

Education in the 1990s: Challenges and Choices

One major reason for the current debate about early academics is that the dramatic increase in maternal employment that occurred in the 1980s has resulted in more and more preschoolers spending large amounts of time every day in preschools or day-care centers. Parents across the spectrum of socioeconomic status are enrolling their young children in early childhood programs and therefore wrestling with the question of whether a play-oriented, child-centered program or a highly structured academic program is best for their children. As Kagan (1990) recently argued, child care for preschoolers and early childhood education arose from very different traditions but are coming to be seen as two facets of the same problem. The basic question is how young children cared for in out-of-home settings can have their "developmental, social, emotional, physical, and cognitive needs" met, within the context of family and community (Kagan, 1990, p. 5).

For the past few years, reports seem to have appeared almost daily in the media about the crisis in American education. Falling Scholastic Aptitude Test scores; rising dropout rates, particularly among minorities; widespread ignorance about geography, math, science, and history found in surveys of high school graduates; the severe shortage of teachers equipped to teach science and math; the dismal performance of American students in academics when compared to Japanese students—these are among the many alarming trends in the American educational system that are forcing us to examine our schools and to search for possible ways to improve them.

Concern over the decline of American education has led to renewed enthusiasm for early intervention programs to help prepare disadvantaged children for school. Federal funding for Head Start has increased dramatically in the past two or three years. Existing Head Start programs are receiving appropriations to increase their enrollments and open new centers. Furthermore, many urban school districts are developing or expanding prekindergarten programs housed in elementary schools. One widely publicized program of this type is New York's Project Giant Step, which in 1989-1990 served approximately sixty-eight hundred low-income preschoolers in four hundred classrooms (Wells, 1990).

Many advocates of mandatory kindergartens and public school for four-year-olds see these programs as crucial to the nation's attempt to revitalize its educational system. Some advocates for academically oriented prekindergarten programs support their views using findings expressed in a National Commission on Excellence in Education (1983) report that emphasized the need for higher academic standards, more rigor in teaching, more emphasis on the "basics," and longer periods of schooling. In contrast, other programs, such as Project Giant Step, are based on a "child-centered philosophy that allows young children to learn through constructive play" and feature a strong parental support component (Wells, 1990).

The debate about early academics has focused primarily on prekindergarten children. However, in recent years, a parallel debate has developed with regard to the issue of the best way to educate children in the primary grades. An increasingly vocal opposition to the "back-to-basics" approach advocates a radically different approach to the education of children in the age range of five to eight. For example, *Newsweek* recently did a long cover story titled "How Kids Learn" (Kantrowitz and Wingert, 1989). In this article, a strong case was made for redesigning the primary grades into environments where young children learn through hands-on experiences, through working cooperatively on theme projects, and through solving problems with concrete materials. The *Newsweek* article quotes the editor of the newsletter of the Council for Basic Education as saying, "The idea of putting small children in front of workbooks and asking them to sit at their desks all day is a nightmare vision" (Kantrowitz and Wingert, 1989, p. 51).

In the "NAEYC Position Statement on Developmentally Appropriate Practice in the Primary Grades Serving 5-Through-8-Year-Olds" (Bredekamp, 1987), officials argue that the curricular content required in the primary grades should be taught so as to build on children's natural interests and talents. The NAEYC approach calls for an integrated curriculum, in which reading and writing might be taught in the context of a social studies project, or math concepts might be covered by studying music. Classroom projects on a major theme (for example, oceans) allow children to work together cooperatively, to explore their own interests, and to develop their basic skills in a stimulating content area. The opportunity for young children to learn through active manipulation of concrete materials is another important element of developmentally appropriate practice according to NAEYC.

A strong case for an "early childhood" approach to education in the primary grades was also made in a report issued by the National Association of State Boards of Education (NASBE, 1988). The twenty-six-member panel that drafted this report criticized the "competitive mentality" driving American education. The report argued that young children are being exposed to formal academic instruction before they are ready. The key recommendation of the report is the formation of "early childhood units" for four-to-eight-year-old children in which rigorous academics, standardized testing, and work sheets are replaced by cooperative learning practices, developmentally appropriate methods and materials, and parent-teacher collaboration.

This emphasis on parent-teacher collaboration stressed in the NASBE task force report reflects an increasing awareness in the field of education that family involvement in children's learning is a crucial ingredient of academic success. For example, research studies of the academic success of Asian-American children consistently refer to the role that parents play in emphasizing education as a value, monitoring homework, and providing supplemental enrichment (Slaughter-Defoe, Nakagawa, Takanishi, and Johnson, 1990; Stevenson, Chen, and Uttal, 1990; Stevenson, Lee, Chen, Stigler, Hsu, and Kitamura, 1990).

One of the most renowned programs to increase parental involvement in schools was developed about twenty years ago by James Comer of Yale University (Comer, 1988). The Comer program has been widely heralded in the media because it is one of the few successful programs designed to significantly improve inner-city schools serving black children. Key elements of the Comer plan are parental involvement in the education process through participation in school governance and management teams, close contact and frequent communication between parent and teacher, and participation in the development of socially relevant curricula (for example, a social skills curriculum focused on such areas as government, business, and health; DeAngelis, 1989).

One of the most important benefits of the early intervention programs of the 1960s was their impact on parents. For example, mothers who participated in the Yale Child Welfare Research Program went on to have fewer children, to complete more education, to obtain more steady employment, and to be more involved in their children's education than did mothers who did not receive this intervention (Seitz, Rosenbaum, and Apfel, 1985). Similarly, children who received the early intervention had fewer school absences, were less likely to be receiving special education services, and had better school adjustment.

Although evidence collected over the last twenty years makes clear that constructive parental involvement in children's learning is a crucial ingredient for academic success, such involvement seems to be declining rather than increasing. Two-career families, the increase in divorce, and the crack epidemic are among the many factors that have widened the gap between school and home. While not as dramatic in its impact as these major sociological factors, another factor contributing to estrangement between home and school may be a discrepancy between how parents and teachers view the process of education. Particularly in regard to young children, parents and teachers who have very different attitudes about what experiences are educational will find it difficult to communicate and collaborate in fostering children's learning.

Just as professionals debate about the best kind of early childhood education, parents also have diverse opinions about the issue of early academic experiences for young children. Many parents feel that it is important to provide preschool children with academic experiences so that they will be prepared for kindergarten. Other parents feel that early academic instruction deprives the young child of the play and socialization experiences so important during the preschool years. The fact that most communities support a wide spectrum of early childhood programs, ranging from the highly academic to the laissez-faire, is one concrete index of a parental "market" for a wide diversity of preschool models.

Conclusion

This chapter has attempted to set the current debate about early academics in historical and sociocultural perspective. In the chapters that follow, a variety of empirical attempts to examine the issue of early academics are described. The topics addressed include what parents actually think about early academic experiences and how parental attitudes translate into choices about schools for their children; what kinds of attitudes preschool teachers hold about early academics and how these attitudes do, or do not, correspond to actual classroom practices; the degree to which the traditional dichotomy between child-centered and teacher-directed programs actually reflects classroom realities; how attitudes about early academics reflect basic conceptions of human development and social values; and the effects that differences in school orientation or practices regarding early academics have on young children's intellectual and emotional development. Finally, this volume addresses some basic issues about the role that early childhood education will play in the United States of the 1990s.

References

Bredekamp, S. E. (ed.). *Developmentally Appropriate Practice in Early Childhood Programs Serving Children from Birth Through Age 8.* Washington, D.C.: National Association for the Education of Young Children, 1987.

Comer, J. P. "Educating Poor Minority Children." *Scientific American,* 1988, 259 (5), 42–48.

DeAngelis, T. "Culture of Failure Mars Disadvantaged Children." *APA Monitor,* 1989, 20, 6, 25.

Doman, G. J. *How to Multiply Your Baby's Intelligence.* Garden City, N.Y.: Doubleday, 1984.

Eastman, P., and Barr, J. L. *Your Child Is Smarter than You Think.* London: Jonathan Cape, 1985.

Elkind, D. *The Hurried Child.* Reading, Mass.: Addison-Wesley, 1981.

Elkind, D. *Miseducation: Preschoolers at Risk.* New York: Knopf, 1987a.

Elkind, D. "Early Childhood Education on Its Own Terms." In S. L. Kagan and E. F. Zigler (eds.), *Early Schooling: The National Debate.* New Haven, Conn.: Yale University Press, 1987b.

Engelmann, S., and Engelmann, T. *Give Your Child a Superior Mind.* New York: Cornerstone, 1981.

Kagan, S. L. *Excellence in Early Childhood Education: Defining Characteristics and Next-Decade Strategies.* Washington, D.C.: U.S. Department of Education, 1990.

Kagan, S. L., and Zigler, E. F. (eds.). *Early Schooling: The National Debate.* New Haven, Conn.: Yale University Press, 1987.

Kantrowitz, B., and Wingert, P. "How Kids Learn." *Newsweek,* Apr. 17, 1989, pp. 50–57.

Ledson, S. *Teach Your Child to Read in 60 Days.* Don Mills, Ontario, Canada: Ontario, 1975.

National Association of State Boards of Education (NASBE). *Right from the Start: Report of the NASBE Task Force on Early Childhood Education.* Alexandria, Va.: NASBE, 1988.

National Commission on Excellence in Education (NCEE). *A Nation At Risk.* Washington, D.C.: NCEE, 1983.

Seitz, V., Rosenbaum, L. K., and Apfel, N. H. "Effects of Family Support Intervention: A Ten-Year Follow-up." *Child Development,* 1985, 56, 376–391.

Sigel, I. E. "Does Hothousing Rob Children of Their Childhood?" *Early Childhood Research Quarterly,* 1987, 2, 211–225.

Slaughter-Defoe, D. T., Nakagawa, K., Takanishi, R., and Johnson, D. J. "Toward Cultural/Ecological Perspectives on Schooling and Achievement in African- and Asian-American Children." *Child Development,* 1990, *61,* 363–383.

Stevenson, H. W., Chen, C., and Uttal, D. H. "Beliefs and Achievement: A Study of Black, White, and Hispanic Children." *Child Development,* 1990, *61,* 518–523.

Stevenson, H. W., Lee, S., Chen, C., Stigler, J. W., Hsu, C., and Kitamura, S. *Contexts of Achievement.* Monographs of the Society for Research in Child Development, vol. 55, no. 1–2 (serial no. 221). Chicago: University of Chicago Press, 1990.

Wells, A. S. "Preschool Program in New York City Is Reported to Surpass Head Start." *New York Times,* May 16, 1990.

Leslie Rescorla is associate professor in the Department of Human Development, Bryn Mawr College, Bryn Mawr, Pennsylvania. She is a clinical and school psychologist with research interests in preschool development, early language delay, childhood psychopathology, and learning disabilities.

What do mothers and preschool teachers think about the value and importance of early academics for prekindergarten children?

Parent and Teacher Attitudes About Early Academics

Leslie Rescorla

In light of the heated media debate about early academics, it is surprising that we know little about how parents and teachers of prekindergarten children view early academic experiences. Although several recent reviews have examined parental attitudes and beliefs about cognitive development (for example, Goodnow, 1988; Miller, 1988), only a few empirical studies are directly pertinent to what parents think about the value and importance of early academic experiences for young children. McGillicuddy-DeLisi (1982), for example, reported that parents of higher socioeconomic status tended to espouse a Rousseauistic view of the child, discounting the benefits of direct instruction and arguing for the idea of developmental readiness. Hess, Kashiwagi, Azuma, Price, and Dickson (1980) did a cross-cultural study of parental expectations for the acquisition of various developmental skills. They found that Japanese parents expected self-control, courtesy, and obedience to develop earlier than did American parents; on the other hand, American parents had earlier timetables for the emergence of verbal assertiveness.

Several studies have also examined variations in teacher attitudes about early academics. For instance, Smith and Shepard (1988) examined the attitudes of kindergarten teachers toward school readiness and found that some teachers espoused an environmentalist view of readiness (with an emphasis on training readiness skills), whereas others expressed a more maturationist perspective (in which readiness skills are seen to take time to appear).

Hess, Price, Dickson, and Conroy (1981) compared parental and teacher attitudes. They asked parents and teachers how much emphasis should be given in preschool to various goals. One major finding was that parents thought school-related skills should be emphasized more and independence skills should be stressed less than did teachers. When the authors compared these responses to how much the same informants believed that such goals were actually stressed in these particular preschools, they found that mothers thought current school emphasis on language, art, and singing skills was somewhat excessive, whereas teachers thought that the schools were placing too great an emphasis on academic skills. Finally, mothers expected children to acquire a variety of developmental skills earlier than did teachers.

In another parent-teacher comparison study, Knudsen-Lindauer and Harris (1989) found that parents were more likely than teachers to expect prekindergarten children to acquire formal academic skills such as counting, reading, and writing before entering school. In contrast, kindergarten teachers rated curiosity and independence as more important qualities for young children than did either mothers or fathers.

Educational Attitude Scale

The instrument described in this chapter—the Educational Attitude Scale (EAS)—was developed in the context of collaborative research known as the Academic Environments study. This research, carried out by Hyson, Hirsh-Pasek, and Rescorla with funding from the Spencer Foundation, was aimed at examining the effects on preschool children of parent and school emphasis on early academic experiences (Hirsh-Pasek, Hyson, and Rescorla, 1990; Hyson, Hirsh-Pasek, and Rescorla, 1990; Hyson, Hirsh-Pasek, Rescorla, Cone, and Martell-Boinske, in press; Rescorla, Hyson, Hirsh-Pasek, and Cone, 1990). We set out to study children whose mothers differed in their attitudes about the value and importance of early academic experiences. We also wanted to assess the attitudes of teachers who were working in what were reputed to be highly academic versus nonacademic early childhood programs. The EAS is the result of our effort to develop a reliable and valid instrument to tap contrasting views about academic instruction for preschool children. We developed two versions of the scale, one for use with parents and another for use with teachers. The teacher version of the EAS is identical in content and format to the parental version, with minor changes in wording to refer to "teacher" as opposed to "parent."

In developing the scale, we felt that it was essential to look at parents' and teachers' academic expectations in the context of their expectations regarding other domains of behavior. Twelve items were formulated to tap views about recognizing and writing letters, numbers, and words. In order to explore attitudes about instruction and enrichment in nonacademic skill areas, we included a four-item athletic domain (swimming and sports) and a four-item arts domain (musical instrument and drawing). We were also interested in parents' and teachers' views about the importance of early social experiences, relative to academic and other skill experiences. Thus, we developed a four-item social domain to tap views about playing and getting along with other children. Finally, we included eight items that assess aspects of behavioral compliance and daily living skills, such as table manners, cleaning up, and trying new foods. We expected that most parents and teachers would strongly support experiences promoting socialization and compliance, but that we would find a wide range of views about experiences in the academic, athletic, and arts skills domains.

All thirty-two EAS items were scored on a 6-point Likert-type scale ranging from "strongly agree" to "strongly disagree." Numerical equivalents for the response categories were constructed so that the maximum score of 6 would always reflect high parental expectations (that is, attitudes favoring instruction and practice in the domains of the scale). Because we wanted to have parents and teachers state whether or not they believe sustained effort and practice are desirable for young children, EAS items were worded to include phrases such as "work at" and "practice at" (for example, "I think preschoolers are too young to practice at playing an instrument"). Similarly, we purposely did not include qualifying terms such as "if he is interested" or "if she wants to." We felt that almost all parents and teachers would agree that any child should be encouraged to play an instrument or learn to read if he or she showed a strong inclination for or interest in this activity, and that only a subset of middle-class adults would endorse such activities in the absence of a child's self-initiated interest.

School Environments

In formulating our research design for the Academic Environments study, we hypothesized that middle-class parents who differed widely in their views about early academic emphasis would select an early childhood program that was consonant with their own values and attitudes. Thus, we collected parent and teacher attitude data from early childhood programs that varied widely with regard to their respective reputations in academic orientation. This allowed us to examine the degree to which parental choices of preschools in terms of academic emphasis correlated with parental attitudes about early academic experiences.

The psychometric data that we collected with the EAS involved two samples of mothers and one sample of teachers. A total of 130 of the 371 mothers responding had four-to-five-year-old children attending one of the eleven early childhood programs participating in our collaborative longitudinal study. The remaining 241 mothers had youngsters attending one of eleven other preschool programs. We recruited this second sample in order to have a sufficiently large number of respondents to examine the psychometric characteristics of the EAS. Finally, twenty-three teachers and directors from the eleven early childhood programs participating in the Academic Environments study completed the teacher version of the EAS.

The twenty-two schools from which we sampled mothers varied widely in philosophy and reputation. At one extreme, we had a small group of mothers who had their children enrolled in a small and very progressive "alternative" school run by educators who carried out "home schooling" with their own children. At the other end of the spectrum, we had a small sample of mothers who had their children enrolled in a widely publicized program that advocates teaching academic skills to infants. In between, we had schools with a strong academic emphasis, including class periods of formal instruction in math, computers, and French; schools in which there was some formal instruction in letters, colors, numbers, and basic readiness skills, mixed in with the more traditional preschool activities; and schools with a strong free-play emphasis and no direct academic instruction ("traditional" nursery schools).

Mothers' Attitudes on the Educational Attitude Scale

Virtually all mothers in the sample felt that social experiences are crucial for young children, as was evident from the high mean and low standard deviation for the four social items that tapped mothers' attitudes about getting along with other children ($M = 5.40$, $SD = .69$). Mothers also felt rather strongly that preschool children should be expected to learn manners, to clean up, and to try new foods (compliance domain: $M = 4.32$, $SD = .61$). The three skill domains presented a sharper difference of opinion. The academic domain manifested both a lower mean and a higher standard deviation ($M = 3.89$, $SD = 1.09$) than found in the social domain. The athletic and arts domains manifested the lowest mean scores ($M = 3.60$ and $M = 3.43$, respectively), indicating that parents in this sample felt that experiences in athletics and art/music are less important for preschoolers than are experiences in the other areas.

When the EAS was divided into two comparable halves, the overall split-half reliability for the scale was .95. Internal consistency of the scale was also high (total alpha = .91). For a sample of thirty-one mothers who completed the EAS twice at one-week intervals, total scale test-retest reliability was .82, with domain reliabilities ranging from .75 for athletic to .83 for academic.

The pattern of intercorrelations between domain scores and total score supported the notion that parents' expectations in the social and compliance domains were independent of their views about the academic, athletic, and arts skill areas. In contrast, there was a relatively high degree of intercorrelation between the three skills domains. Total score on the EAS was best correlated with the academic domain ($r = .92$). Scores in the athletic and arts domains were also highly correlated with total score ($r = .71$ and $r = .73$, respectively), whereas the social and compliance domains were less closely associated with total score ($r = .40$ and $r = .56$, respectively). When the EAS was submitted to factor analysis, it appeared that the first major factor consisted of all twelve academic items, the second major factor contained all the social and most of the compliance items, and the third large factor contained the athletic and arts items.

Relationship Between Parent and Teacher Attitudes

At the beginning of our collaborative project, we had made informal classifications of all eleven programs in the Academic Environments study according to their community reputations for academic emphasis. Six schools were rated as "high academic" in emphasis and five schools were rated as "low academic" in orientation. The data that we collected using the teacher version of the EAS with twenty-three teachers and directors in ten of these schools enabled us to determine whether our impressions about the degree of academic emphasis of each school, based on our knowledge of their community reputations, were in fact accurate representations of each school's philosophy.

Analysis of our data revealed that mothers and teachers in both high-academic and low-academic preschools agreed that social experiences are important for preschoolers and that adults should have expectations for young children in behavioral areas such as cleaning up and displaying good manners. The data also revealed that teachers and parents in high-academic schools differed in their views about early skill experiences from teachers and parents in low-academic schools. Early childhood programs with a community reputation for being high in academic orientation had mothers and teachers who shared a belief in the value of academic, athletic, and arts activities for young children. In contrast, schools with a community reputation for being play-oriented and nonacademic in focus had mothers and teachers who felt that early skill experiences were much less important.

Our final analysis consisted of a comparison of parent and teacher attitudes about early experiences. This analysis revealed that parents had significantly higher expectations and placed more value on early skill experiences than did their children's teachers. This pattern of parents having higher skill expectations than their children's teachers was especially evident in the low-academic schools. Thus, mothers consistently placed more value on the importance of early academic, athletic, and arts experiences than did teachers, with maternal attitudes more discrepant from teacher attitudes in the low-academic than in the high-academic preschools.

Conclusion

In conclusion, the EAS proved to be a reliable and valid tool for measuring parent and teacher attitudes about early academic experiences. We found that parents who held very similar attitudes about the importance of social experiences for young children differed widely in their attitudes about early academic instruction. Furthermore, our research showed that parents who placed a strong value on early academics sent their children to schools with a community reputation for academic emphases, schools in which the teachers also thought that early academics are important. Finally, consistent with the findings of Hess, Price, Dickson, and Conroy (1981) and of Knudsen-Lindauer and Harris (1989), it appeared that there were significant discrepancies between maternal attitudes and teachers' views in the schools where they had enrolled their children, with mothers consistently placing greater value than did the teachers on early skills experiences. The parent-teacher discrepancy was particularly evident in schools with community reputations for being low-academic, that is, play-oriented and unstructured in classroom practices.

In planning the Academic Environments study, we decided to examine the issue of early academics in upper-middle-class families—families with disposable incomes and educational backgrounds that enabled them to choose early childhood programs in a highly selective manner. However, we are very interested in extending this work across a broader socioeconomic spectrum. Specifically, we plan to examine the utility of the EAS in research on parental attitudes in less economically advantaged families. We are interested in looking at how less highly educated parents regard early academic experiences for their prekindergarten children—children for whom educational success may be the crucial factor determining upward social mobility. Similarly, we would like to investigate how different ethnic and racial minority groups respond to the EAS. Finally, we intend to investigate teacher attitudes on the EAS as a function of their employment settings (nursery school, day-care center, Head Start, independent school). Such future studies will allow us to examine parent and teacher attitudes about early academics in a broader sociocultural context.

References

Goodnow, J. "Parents' Ideas, Actions, and Feelings: Models and Methods from Developmental and Social Psychology." *Child Development,* 1988, *59,* 286–320.

Hess, R. D., Kashiwagi, K., Azuma, H., Price, G. G., and Dickson, W. P. "Maternal Expectations for Mastery of Developmental Tasks in Japan and the United States." *International Journal of Psychology,* 1980, *15,* 259–271.

Hess, R. D., Price, G. G., Dickson, W. P., and Conroy, M. "Different Roles for Mothers and Teachers: Contrasting Styles of Child Care." In S. Kilmer (ed.), *Advances in Early Education and Day Care.* Vol. 2. Greenwich, Conn.: JAI, 1981.

Hirsh-Pasek, K., Hyson, M. C., and Rescorla, L. "Academic Environments in Preschool: Challenge or Pressure?" *Early Education and Development,* 1990, *1* (6), 401–423.

Hyson, M. C., Hirsh-Pasek, K., and Rescorla, L. "The Classroom Practices Inventory: An Observational Instrument Based on NAEYC's Guidelines for Developmentally

Appropriate Practices for 4- and 5-Year-Old Children." *Early Childhood Research Quarterly,* 1990, *5,* 475–494.

Hyson, M. C., Hirsh-Pasek, K., Rescorla, L., Cone, J., and Martell-Boinske, L. "Ingredients of Parental 'Pressure' in Early Childhood." *Journal of Applied Developmental Psychology,* in press.

Knudsen-Lindauer, S., and Harris, K. "Priorities for Kindergarten Curricula: Views of Parents and Teachers." *Journal of Research on Childhood Education,* 1989, 4 (1), 51–61.

McGillicuddy-DeLisi, A. V. "Parental Beliefs About Developmental Processes." *Human Development,* 1982, 25, 195–200.

Miller, S. A. "Parents' Beliefs About Children's Cognitive Development." *Child Development,* 1988, 59, 259–285.

Rescorla, L., Hyson, M. C., Hirsh-Pasek, K., and Cone, J. "Academic Expectations in Mothers of Preschool Children: A Psychometric Study of the Educational Attitude Scale." *Early Education and Development,* 1990, 1 (3), 165–184.

Smith, M. L., and Shepard, L. A. "Kindergarten Readiness and Retention: A Qualitative Study of Teachers' Beliefs and Practices." *American Educational Research Journal,* 1988, 25, 307–333.

Leslie Rescorla is associate professor in the Department of Human Development, Bryn Mawr College, Bryn Mawr, Pennsylvania. She is a clinical and school psychologist with research interests in preschool development, early language delay, childhood psychopathology, and learning disabilities.

*Academic preschools have been caricatured in the popular press;
what are these preschools really like, and to what extent are they
created by teachers?*

The Characteristics and Origins of the Academic Preschool

Marion C. Hyson

Academic preschools are not new, nor is the debate over their appropriateness. Although mainstream early childhood education programs have usually advocated playful learning, the history of early childhood education contains many examples of formal, academically focused programs for young children (Spodek, 1982; Strickland, 1982). In the early 1900s, opponents attacked American kindergartens for their rigid interpretation of the philosophy of the influential German educator Friedrich Froebel (Weber, 1969). Early intervention programs of the 1960s included attempts to implement formal academic curricula, most notably represented by Bereiter and Engelmann's (1966) controversial "academically oriented preschool."

While there have always been some academically oriented preschools, their number grew to unprecedented levels during the 1980s. In contrast to the academic intervention programs of the 1960s, these programs have appeared in diverse settings and serve families from every income level.

The popular press has created a portrait—or, some would say, a caricature—of the contemporary "academic preschool," attended by briefcase-laden tots and staffed by drill masters intent on preparing their four-year-old charges for Harvard. In this chapter I try to take a more objective, empirical look at the phenomenon. I review some methods for observing and describing academic preschool programs, with an emphasis on observations conducted as part of the Academic Environments study (Hyson and Hirsh-Pasek, 1989). I also discuss relationships between classroom practices and teachers' beliefs about appropriate early education.

New Directions for Child Development, no. 53, Fall 1991 © Jossey-Bass Inc., Publishers

Measuring the Features of an "Academic Preschool"

Systematic observational studies of teaching practices and curricula in academic preschools are still rare. However, some of the earlier classroom observation research contains potentially helpful findings. Many analytical instruments developed in the 1960s and early 1970s (Simon and Boyer, 1967; Soar and Soar, 1982) emphasized the contrast between teacher-dominated practices and those that encourage autonomy and child-initiated learning (for example, Flanders, 1970). These observation systems, however, were designed for use in elementary schools. Because most rely on classification of verbal behavior, they may be less informative when used to observe younger, less verbal children.

Within early childhood education, several observation systems were devised in the 1980s as part of research projects examining early childhood program quality. One example is Harms and Clifford's (1980) Early Childhood Environment Rating Scale (ECERS), which is frequently used in daycare research (Whitebook, Howes, and Phillips, 1989). An "academic" preschool would receive low ratings on a number of ECERS items because of a lack of open-ended play materials and overemphasis on whole-group instruction. Similarly, the National Association for the Education of Young Children (NAEYC) has developed an observation system for use in accrediting high-quality early childhood programs (Bredekamp, 1986). In this scale, lower ratings would be received by programs emphasizing use of abstract paper-and-pencil activities and direct, whole-group teaching of academic skills.

Although they contain items appropriate for identifying formal academic programs, none of the above measures was designed specifically for that purpose. More recently, a very few researchers have devised observation instruments to study academic instruction in kindergarten and, to a lesser extent, in preschool (Burts, Hart, Charlesworth, and Kirk, 1990; Durkin, 1987; Smith and Shepard, 1988; Stipek, this volume). A few examples illustrate the approaches that are being taken.

An ongoing program of research at Louisiana State University has focused on the effect of academically oriented kindergartens on the stress behaviors and achievement levels of young children. These researchers have devised a self-report questionnaire for kindergarten teachers in which the teachers describe their instructional practices. The items are designed to highlight the use of "inappropriate" or formally academic practices (for example, "practicing handwriting on lines"). A parallel observation measure was developed to allow observers to validate these descriptions with classroom ratings (Burts, Hart, Charlesworth, and Kirk, 1990; Charlesworth, Hart, Burts, and Hernandez, in press).

Stipek (this volume) has also been examining the effect of different instructional strategies on kindergarten and preschool children's behavior and emotions. Stipek employs a time-sampling observational approach that identifies the frequency of various classroom activities (for example, paper-and-pencil academic tasks). Observers also record how the classroom is organized at various points during the day (whole-group instruction, independent seat work, and so on).

When we began the Academic Environments study, instruments did not exist for the study of prekindergarten academic programs. Because of this need, the Classroom Practices Inventory (CPI) was developed. As a starting point, we turned to NAEYC's guidelines for developmentally appropriate practice (Bredekamp, 1987). The CPI (Hyson, Hirsh-Pasek, and Rescorla, 1990) operationalizes a subset of the NAEYC guidelines. As detailed in Hyson, Hirsh-Pasek, and Rescorla (1990), the CPI asks the classroom observer to rate each of twenty-six statements on a 5-point Likert-type scale, from "not at all like this classroom" to "very much like this classroom." Twenty of the items specifically describe program characteristics; half of these items (the "inappropriate program" items, as NAEYC termed them) were consistent with anecdotal descriptions of an academically focused classroom. (For example, "Teachers expect children to respond correctly with one right answer. Memorization and drill are emphasized"; "Art projects involve copying an adult-made model . . . or following other adult directions"; "Reading and writing instruction emphasizes direct teaching of letter recognition, reciting the alphabet, coloring within the lines, and being instructed in the correct formation of letters.") The remaining ten program items, written in parallel form, are more consistent with a child-initiated, "developmentally appropriate" approach. (For example, "Teachers ask questions which encourage children to give more than one right answer"; "Children use a variety of art media, including easel and finger painting, in ways of their choosing"; "The classroom environment encourages children to listen to and read stories, dictate stories, notice print in use in the classroom, engage in dramatic play, experiment with writing." An additional six items were written to assess the program's emotional climate. Again, half of these items were written in positive or "appropriate" form (for example, "Teachers talk about feelings"); the others describe more unemotional, critical, or punitive practices (for example, "Teachers use competition, comparison, or criticism as discipline techniques").

Staff from the Academic Environments project observed and rated ten preschool classrooms, including five reputed to be "academic" preschools and five others reputed to be much more child-centered and unstructured. Observers visited each program for three hours on at least two occasions. Two observers visited each program; CPI scores correlated .86 across pairs of raters.

The measure was designed so that by reversing the scoring on the "low-academic" or "developmentally appropriate" items, a mean "academic emphasis" score could be obtained. The lower the score (on a 1-to-5 scale), the more the classroom would be characterized by teacher-directed, academically focused practices.

Academic Preschools' Reputations Versus Reality

Direct observations of the ten classrooms confirmed their community reputations. The five reputedly academic programs had significantly lower CPI scores ($M = 2.24$) than those reputed to be less geared toward academics ($M = 3.94$).

Specific teaching practices said to be typical of the "academic preschool" tended to co-occur. Classrooms with higher ratings on the "academic program" CPI items were very unlikely to have high ratings on the "low-academic" or play-oriented items (as identified in Exhibit 3.1). Like oil and water, workbooks and blocks do not mix in practice. In addition, classrooms with a strong academic program emphasis had a significantly less positive emotional climate (Hyson, Hirsh-Pasek, and Rescorla, 1990).

Further confirmation of these patterns was gained from a factor analysis of the scale using 207 separate observations of fifty-eight programs, including the ten in the Academic Environments study (Hyson, Hirsh-Pasek, and Rescorla, 1990). Over half of the variance was accounted for by the first factor, which loaded highly on items that tap the encouragement of creativity and curiosity through use of concrete, open-ended materials and divergent teacher questions. The second factor, in contrast, loaded most heavily on those items having to do with workbooks, drill, and isolated skills. The "emotional climate" items formed a third factor, and the fourth factor had high loadings on items rating physical activity and child choice. (Further information about the measure's psychometric properties are in Hyson, Hirsh-Pasek, and Rescorla, 1990.)

Academic Preschools and Teachers' Educational Attitudes

Are teachers' practices consistent with their attitudes toward early academics? A few studies have examined the "belief-behavior" connection in

Exhibit 3.1. Classroom Practices Inventory Items

Part One: Program/Activity Focus
1. Children select their own activities from a variety of learning areas the teacher prepares, including dramatic play, blocks, science, math, games and puzzles, books, recordings, art, and music. (A)
2. Large-group, teacher-directed instruction is used most of the time. Children are doing the same things at the same time. (I)
3. Children are involved in concrete, three-dimensional learning activities, with materials closely related to children's daily life experiences. (A)
4. The teacher tells the children exactly what they will do and when. The teacher expects the children to follow his or her plans. (I)

Exhibit 3.1. (continued)

5. Children are physically active in the classroom, choosing from activities the teacher has set up and spontaneously initiating many of their own activities. (A)
6. Children work individually or in small, child-chosen groups most of the time. Different children are doing different things. (A)
7. Children use workbooks, ditto sheets, flashcards, or other abstract or two-dimensional learning materials. (I)
8. Teachers ask questions that encourage children to give more than one right answer. (A)
9. Teachers expect children to sit down, watch, be quiet, and listen, or do paper-and-pencil tasks for major periods of time. (I)
10. Reading and writing instruction emphasizes direct teaching of letter recognition, reciting the alphabet, coloring within the lines, and being instructed in the correct formation of letters. (I)
11. Teachers use activities such as block building, measuring ingredients for cooking, woodworking, and drawing to help children learn concepts in math, science, and social studies. (A)
12. Children have planned lessons in writing with pencils, coloring predrawn forms, tracing, or correctly using scissors. (I)
13. Children use a variety of art media, including easel and finger painting and clay, in ways of their choosing. (A)
14. Teachers expect children to respond correctly with one right answer. Memorization and drill are emphasized. (I)
15. When teachers try to get children involved in activities, they do so by stimulating children's natural curiosity and interest. (A)
16. The classroom environment encourages children to listen to and read stories, dictate stories, notice print in use in the classroom, engage in dramatic play, experiment with writing by drawing, copying, and inventing their own spelling. (A)
17. Art projects involve copying an adult-made model, coloring predrawn forms, finishing a project the teacher has started, or following other adult directions. (I)
18. Separate times or periods are set aside to learn material in specific content areas such as math, science, or social studies. (I)
19. Children have daily opportunities to use pegboards, puzzles, legos, markers, scissors, or other similar materials in ways the children choose. (A)
20. When teachers try to get children involved in activities, they do so by requiring their participation, giving rewards, disapproving of failure to participate, and so on. (I)

Part Two: Emotional Climate
1. Teachers show affection by smiling at, touching, and holding children and speaking to them at their eye level throughout the day, but especially at arrival and departure times. (A)
2. The sound of the environment is marked by pleasant conversation, spontaneous laughter, and exclamations of excitement. (A)
3. Teachers use competition, comparison, or criticism as guidance or discipline techniques. (I)
4. Teachers talk about feelings. They encourage children to put their emotions (positive and negative) and ideas into words. (A)
5. The sound of the environment is characterized either by harsh noise or enforced quiet. (I)
6. Teachers use redirection, positive reinforcement, and encouragement as guidance or discipline techniques. (A)

Note: (A) = appropriate practice for four- and five-year-old children, (I) = inappropriate practice for four- and five-year-old children.

preschool and kindergarten settings. Smith and Shepard (1988) found that kindergarten teachers who held strong beliefs in the power of direct teaching, remediation, or intervention were less likely to retain children at the end of kindergarten than were kindergarten teachers with more "nativist" beliefs. In Burts, Hart, Charlesworth, Fleege, Mosley, and Thomasson's (in press) study, nineteen out of twenty kindergarten teachers were observed to have classroom practices congruent with their self-reported beliefs in developmentally appropriate curriculum. Wing (1989) interviewed preschool directors about their beliefs concerning early skill-based reading and writing instruction and found that these beliefs were reflected in teachers' observed practices.

In order to investigate this belief-behavior connection, we correlated CPI scores with preschoolers' mean scores on the teacher version of the Educational Attitude Scale (EAS) (Rescorla, Hyson, Hirsh-Pasek, and Cone, 1990). This thirty-two-item measure reflects teachers' self-reported beliefs about early academics and adult-directed learning. This analysis showed substantial consistency between direct observation of academically related classroom practices and the self-reported educational attitudes of the staff. Those programs with staff who espoused beliefs in teacher-directed, formal academic learning were rated by observers as significantly more academically focused than were programs with staff who espoused beliefs in child-initiated, play-oriented learning (Spearman r (10) = -.61, $p < .001$).

Teachers' Beliefs and Practices: Understanding the Relationship

This finding suggests that the contemporary "academic preschool" has been created by teachers who believe in the value of early academic training. However, there are reasons to question this relationship between teacher beliefs and program orientation.

First, as noted by Rescorla (this volume [Chapter Two]), in our study teachers never endorsed early academics as strongly as did parents, when parents and teachers at the same preschools were compared. One might hypothesize that the leading role in promoting the academic preschool is occupied not by early childhood educators but by parents.

Second, the direction of effects in the teacher belief-behavior association may be questioned. Although it is reasonable to think that teachers' educational attitudes determine their classroom practices, practices may also change attitudes. If a teacher is employed by a highly academic preschool, his or her educational beliefs may become more congruent with mandated classroom practices.

Third, in our study the correlation between teachers' educational attitudes and their classroom practices, although statistically significant, was far from perfect. A number of teachers who rejected formal academic beliefs on the EAS still ran high-academic classrooms.

What accounts for the teachers with play beliefs and workbook practices? As recent discussions of "reflective practice" (Schön, 1983) and some empirical studies (Campbell, 1985; Hatch and Freeman, 1988; Smith and Shepard, 1988) have emphasized, many factors influence teachers' classroom behavior.

Some teachers may feel pressured to act in opposition to their beliefs. Kindergarten teachers often respond to expectations to "teach to the tests" that will be given early in first grade. Administrators often endorse more emphasis on early formal academics than what the teachers really wish to supply. One teacher took us aside to say that although she went along with the director's curriculum (which included scissor-cutting lessons and handwriting practice for four-year-olds), she did so only because she had needed a job, and she was planning to quit at the end of the year.

Other teachers may feel pressured to endorse anti-academic beliefs because of the social desirability of these beliefs. All the major professional organizations in early childhood education have opposed formal academic instruction and have widely publicized their opposition. The teacher who covertly opposes the conventional wisdom may be reluctant to express those ideas on an attitude survey. In this case, observed classroom practices may be a more accurate index of a teacher's beliefs.

A truer picture of early childhood educators' attitudes toward the academic preschool might be obtained through qualitative interviews that tap teachers' "case knowledge" rather than through rating their agreement with a series of abstract propositions. Smith and Shepard (1988) productively used this interview approach with kindergarten teachers and the method could easily be adapted for other research.

Many early childhood education professionals believe that the recent trend toward a more formally academic preschool curriculum should be reversed. Teachers are a key element in this process. Our research and that of others suggests that, although there is some support among some teachers for formal academic instruction in preschool, this support is far from universal. Many early childhood teachers appear to be living with inconsistency between what they believe is good for children and what they are doing in the classroom. The academically focused preschool is by no means a simple product of teachers who believe in academics and plan a curriculum around these beliefs. Rather, the observed classroom environment is the product of a network of influences, including parental expectations, administrative dictates, and broad societal imperatives. Any attempt to return preschools to a more child-centered focus must take these interconnected influences into account.

References

Bereiter, C., and Engelmann, S. *Teaching Disadvantaged Children in the Preschool.* Englewood Cliffs, N.J.: Prentice-Hall, 1966.

Bredekamp, S. E. "The Reliability and Validity of the Early Childhood Classroom Observation Scale for Accrediting Early Childhood Programs." *Early Childhood Research Quarterly*, 1986, *1*, 103–108.

Bredekamp, S. E. (ed.). *Developmentally Appropriate Practice in Early Childhood Programs Serving Children from Birth Through Age 8*. Washington, D.C.: National Association for the Education of Young Children, 1987.

Burts, D. C., Hart, C. H., Charlesworth, R., Fleege, P. O., Mosley, J., and Thomasson, R. H. "Observed Activities and Stress Behaviors of Children in Developmentally Appropriate and Inappropriate Kindergarten Classrooms." *Early Childhood Research Quarterly*, in press.

Burts, D. C., Hart, C. H., Charlesworth, R., and Kirk, L. "A Comparison of Frequencies of Stress Behaviors Observed in Kindergarten Children in Classrooms with Developmentally Appropriate Versus Developmentally Inappropriate Instructional Practices." *Early Childhood Research Quarterly*, 1990, *5*, 407–423.

Campbell, C. "Variables Which Influence Student-Teacher Behavior: Implications for Teacher Education." *Alberta Journal of Educational Research*, 1985, *31*, 258–269.

Charlesworth, R., Hart, C. H., Burts, D. C., and Hernandez, S. "Identifying Kindergarten Beliefs and Practices: A Questionnaire Approach." *Early Child Development and Care*, in press.

Durkin, D. "A Classroom-Observation Study of Reading Instruction in Kindergarten." *Early Childhood Research Quarterly*, 1987, *2*, 275–300.

Flanders, N. *Analyzing Teacher Behavior*. Reading, Mass.: Addison-Wesley, 1970.

Harms, T., and Clifford, R. M. *Early Childhood Environment Rating Scale*. New York: Teachers College Press, 1980.

Hatch, J. A., and Freeman, E. B. "Kindergarten Philosophies and Practices: Perspectives of Teachers, Principals, and Supervisors." *Early Childhood Research Quarterly*, 1988, *3*, 151–166.

Hyson, M. C., and Hirsh-Pasek, K. "Academic Environments in Early Childhood: Challenge or Pressure?" Unpublished final report to the Spencer Foundation, Chicago, 1989.

Hyson, M. C., Hirsh-Pasek, K., and Rescorla, L. "The Classroom Practices Inventory: An Observational Instrument Based on NAEYC's Guidelines for Developmentally Appropriate Practices for 4- and 5-Year-Old Children." *Early Childhood Research Quarterly*, 1990, *5*, 475–494.

Rescorla, L., Hyson, M. C., Hirsh-Pasek, K., and Cone, J. "Academic Expectations in Mothers of Preschool Children: A Psychometric Study of the Educational Attitude Scale." *Early Education and Development*, 1990, *1* (3), 165–184.

Schön, D. A. *The Reflective Practitioner*. New York: Basic Books, 1983.

Simon, A., and Boyer, E. G. (eds.). *Mirrors of Behavior: An Anthology of Classroom Observation Instruments*. Philadelphia: Research for Better Schools, 1967.

Smith, M. L., and Shepard, L. A. "Kindergarten Readiness and Retention: A Qualitative Study of Teachers' Beliefs and Practices." *American Educational Research Journal*, 1988, *25*, 307–333.

Soar, R. S., and Soar, R. M. "Measurement of Classroom Process." In B. Spodek (ed.), *Handbook of Research in Early Childhood Education*. New York: Free Press, 1982.

Spodek, B. (ed.). *Handbook of Research in Early Childhood Education*. New York: Free Press, 1982.

Strickland, C. E. "Paths Not Taken: Seminal Models of Early Childhood Education in Jacksonian America." In B. Spodek (ed.), *Handbook of Research in Early Childhood Education*. New York: Free Press, 1982.

Weber, E. *The Kindergarten: Its Encounter with Educational Thought in America.* New York: Teachers College Press, 1969.

Whitebook, M., Howes, C., and Phillips, D. *Who Cares? Child Care Teachers and the Quality of Care in America.* Final Report of the National Child Care Staffing Study. Oakland, Calif.: Child Care Employee Project, 1989.

Wing, L. A. "The Influence of Preschool Teachers' Beliefs on Young Children's Conceptions of Reading and Writing." *Early Childhood Research Quarterly,* 1989, 4, 61–74.

Marion C. Hyson is associate professor in the Department of Individual and Family Studies, University of Delaware, Newark, specializing in early childhood education and early emotional development.

Mothers have many possible ways of "building a hothouse":
selecting an academic preschool, enrolling their child in lessons,
and using highly directive, controlling patterns of interaction.

Building the Hothouse: How Mothers Construct Academic Environments

Marion C. Hyson

If the hothousing phenomenon is real, someone must be building the hot-house. In the last decade, there has been renewed interest in the interpersonal context of child development (Bronfenbrenner, 1979; Maccoby and Martin, 1983; Vygotsky, 1978; Wertsch, 1985). As Valsiner (1987) points out, parents in all cultures constrain and channel children's development into directions consistent with family and cultural values. We might think of parents as developmental general contractors. Guided by plans that are subject to revision, they coordinate various phases of the developmental "project," delegating some tasks to others but maintaining overall control of the process.

Using data primarily from the Academic Environments project (Hyson and Hirsh-Pasek, 1989), this chapter examines parental actions that contribute to the construction of hothousing environments. First, I discuss parents' constructions of out-of-home hothouses where their children spend time when not under direct parental supervision. Next, I describe processes through which parents construct "home hothouses," using family activities and interactions. Finally, I examine the affective climate of the hothouse. Popular writers have assumed that there is a prototypical "pushy parent"—anxious, perfectionistic, and driven to place unrealistic demands on small children. I assess the validity of that stereotype.

The Hothouse Away from Home

Parents' raw materials for building hothouses away from home include various kinds of preschool programs and other organized activities for young children.

Selecting a Preschool Program. Middle- and upper-middle-class parents generally have choices about the early childhood programs in which they enroll their children. Parents can structure their young child's day-to-day environment by choosing a preschool whose philosophy is consistent with their educational beliefs. As noted in an earlier chapter (Rescorla, this volume [Chapter Two]), parents in the Academic Environments study generally selected preschool programs that were consistent with their "hothousing beliefs" as indexed by the Educational Attitude Scale (EAS).

In our interviews with 125 mothers of four-year-olds, my colleagues and I asked why they had chosen their children's preschools. The mothers usually gave detailed reasons, citing the fit of the programs with their respective educational philosophies and with their perceptions of the children's needs. The following comments are characteristic of those mothers whose EAS scores reflected a "low-academic" or play orientation: "There is not the pressure that you find in other schools around. . . . Our main concern in picking the school was just for the kids to learn to interact and play with other children, as opposed to getting into kindergarten and knowing how to read. That is just not that important to us right now." "I wanted a warm, nurturing kind of environment; I wanted a place where he would be loved. . . . It was noncompetitive; I wasn't concerned about academics—that wasn't important to me in the preschool years at all." In contrast, another mother, who held strong "pro-hothousing" beliefs, explained her choice of a preschool program as follows: "Well, I chose it [because] they needed a structured situation, I thought; I didn't want them to be playing all the time." Another "pro-hothousing" mother stated, "I was looking for a preschool that was a little bit more than just two-and-a-half hours of free play; something a little bit more structured, that would make use of this year." Thus, each of the middle-class mothers in the Academic Environments study viewed the selection of a preschool as much more than finding a pleasant place for her child to spend a few hours a week.

Organized Activities for Young Children. "She takes dance class; it's just a pre-ballet, creative movement. And they're taking skating lessons this winter, and in the summertime they take swimming lessons. And this summer, um, well last summer, well for five years, she has taken some gym classes and classes at the community arts center." Years ago, children were expected to learn economically useful skills such as planting, weaving, or tending animals. Now, middle-class parents enroll their children in organized programs of instruction in music, art, sports, and so on. Children generally begin these lessons in elementary school; indeed, developmental psychologists have viewed children's spontaneous interest in adult-organized instruction as a cognitive and psychosocial landmark in the transition to middle childhood (for example, Erikson, 1950; Minuchin, 1977). Preschool children once were considered too young to profit from formal "lessons." In recent years, however, classes for very young children have proliferated.

In the Academic Environments study, mothers were questioned about their children's activities. Although all the children in our study were attending preschool for at least part of every weekday, the majority were also enrolled in out-of-school classes. If a child attended any out-of-school class, we asked the mother why she had enrolled the child. These mothers were often quite direct about introducing the idea of extracurricular lessons to their children and "shopping" for activities that would use their children's time well: "I thought it would be good for her—it [the original idea] was me." "I basically took the initiative and discussed it with her. That [tumbling] was something she wanted to try."

We asked each mother how her child liked the classes he or she was taking. Many mothers reported entirely positive attitudes: "She went to a gymnastics school . . . and she adored it; she just had a wonderful time. . . . She always was anxious to go, you know, and she liked getting her little leotards on."

However, quite a few mothers acknowledged that their children did not care for out-of-school lessons, at least at first. Some mothers quickly dropped lessons if their children did not take to them, while others pressed forward and claimed that their children enjoyed the lessons more as time went on: "She's taking piano lessons right now. . . . The first time [we tried piano lessons] she decided to forget it but now she's enjoying it." "We tried karate because he's interested in that, but they [karate instructors] thought he was a little too young for that, so we are going to try that again, probably in September."

These out-of-home activities, like the children's preschools, were selected by mothers to develop children's skills and interests, and to prepare the children for even more organized programs of instruction in the future. Of course, there were mothers who did not choose to enroll their children in these activities. Some simply felt their children were too young; others felt that the preschools included enough enrichment activities. For example, many schools offered special classes in swimming, gymnastics, music, and foreign languages. Such classes were usually mentioned approvingly by the mothers.

The Hothouse at Home

Although the children in the Academic Environments study were involved in out-of-home activities selected by the parents, they also spent time with their mothers at home. Here, too, mothers had opportunities to channel children's interests in desired directions.

Although home observations were not feasible, we were able to videotape ninety mother-child dyads from the Academic Environments sample during two activities that assessed the mother's style of teaching and interacting with her child. We were especially interested in the mothers' use of directives and the methods of control and criticism often associated with the hothousing phenomenon.

First, each mother-child dyad was asked to copy a series of increasingly difficult designs using an Etch-a-Sketch toy, with the mother controlling one knob and the child the other. Mothers' verbal directiveness, criticism, questioning strategies, and negative emotion were coded from transcripts. In addition, we looked at variations in perfectionism, as measured by how many tries the pair took before deciding that the designs were "good enough."

The second task was more open-ended. Mother and child were given a set of colorful geometrical stickers with which to make a picture together. Again, maternal directiveness, criticism, and questioning were coded. In addition, maternal control was rated, based on the videotapes; mothers receiving higher control scores were those who dominated the decisions about what kinds of pictures to make, which stickers to use, when the pictures were finished, and so on. (Details of procedures and measures for both tasks are in Hyson, Hirsh-Pasek, Rescorla, Cone, and Martell-Boinske, in press).

Mothers varied a great deal in their use of hothousing techniques. Some mothers were strikingly directive, even in the picture-making task:

MOTHER: What are you going to do with them? There has to be a plan!
    What are you going to do?
CHILD: Now . . . now we need grass.
MOTHER: The yellow doesn't look like grass.

Other mothers employed a more collaborative technique, allowing the children to use their own ideas, as shown in this example from the more structured Etch-a-Sketch task:

MOTHER: Are you going to go across, there?
CHILD: [nods]
MOTHER: Okay. Maybe we can go up. You were right.
CHILD: Yeah! We did it.

Mothers appeared fairly consistent in their use of hothousing actions. For example, during the stickers task mothers who frequently used verbal commands also used significantly more critical comments and fewer open-ended questions, and they were rated as significantly more controlling. Although the two tasks were quite different, resulting in varying amounts of adult directiveness, we found that mothers who used many commands in the stickers task tended to do the same in the Etch-a-Sketch task, and that mothers' controlling behavior during the stickers task was correlated with more criticism in the Etch-a-Sketch task (Hyson, Hirsh-Pasek, Rescorla, Cone, and Martin-Boinske, in press).

We also found that mothers' attitudes about adult instruction and early academics were somewhat predictive of their use of hothousing actions six months later. On the basis of their standardized scores on the EAS and the Developmental Expectations Card Sort, we identified twenty-three strongly "pro-hothousing" mothers. These mothers used significantly more commands and exerted more control during the mother-child tasks than did the twenty-seven "anti-hothousing" mothers. This pattern is similar to that found in several other studies in which parents' authoritarian or direct-instruction beliefs were expressed in a more direct, less developmentally sensitive interactive style, especially during unstructured tasks (Pratt, Kerig, Cowan, and Cowan, 1988; Segal, 1985; Sigel and McGillicuddy-DeLisi, 1984; Skinner, 1985).

Affective Climate of the Hothouse

To many writers, the hothousing phenomenon includes more than early instruction or emphasis on formal academics; it also connotes an atmosphere of pressure, anxiety, and perfectionism. The Academic Environments study assessed this affective climate through interviewer ratings of mothers' characteristics, including rigidity, anxiety, and critical attitude toward their children. This "pressure rating" from the interview correlated significantly with mothers' pro-hothousing beliefs. High-pressure ratings also predicted mothers' use of negative emotion and criticism during the mother-child tasks, although all of these correlations were modest in size (Hyson, Hirsh-Pasek, Rescorla, Cone, and Martell-Boinske, in press).

Putting the Plan Together

The preceding discussion suggests considerable coherence among mothers' hothousing plans and a number of maternal actions and affective characteristics. To further investigate these relationships, we used a cluster analysis procedure, including nine variables that indexed maternal hothousing beliefs, the academic emphasis of the preschool that the parents selected for the child (Hyson, this volume), mothers' controlling behavior in the interactive tasks, and interviewer ratings of mothers' affective characteristics (Hyson and Hirsh-Pasek, 1989). Although the magnitude of the group differences is a function of the clustering procedure, the pattern of differences on these variables is interesting.

A two-group solution produced a group of mothers (about one-third of the entire sample) whose pattern of scores appears to embody the beliefs, actions, and affect of the so-called hothousing parent. As compared with the contrasting cluster of mothers, this group had higher academic expectations and earlier timetables for developmental skills. These mothers chose more academically focused preschools, and they were more controlling, critical, and negative in interactions with their children. This cluster of mothers also received higher ratings on anxiety, rigidity, and criticism.

To see if the groups could be further differentiated, we examined a three-group cluster solution using the same variables. This solution again produced contrasting "high" and "low" hothousing mothers with patterns of scores similar to those described above. Eight mothers formed a third group, which consisted of parents who had been classified in the low-hothousing cluster in the two-group solution. These mothers were distinctive because, although they professed anti-hothousing beliefs and sent their children to play-oriented preschools, they showed high levels of criticism and perfectionist behavior during the mother-child tasks.

Conclusion

The preceding discussion underscores the many ways in which parents may implement their ideas about desirable environments for young children. The mothers in our study showed a great deal of planning and consistency. Those who believed in early adult-directed instruction and high performance standards marshaled out-of-home activities to support those beliefs and brought a notable degree of directiveness to bear on their children even in "playful" tasks like making a picture.

Lest this picture be oversimplified, I must emphasize that a statistical degree of consistency does not mean that every mother with high expectations fit the full-blown hothousing stereotype. As the cluster analysis showed, even apparently "laid back" mothers could be anxious and critical at times. Furthermore, the degree of association among our categories of hothousing actions was very modest. Like other belief-behavior studies, our significant correlations were typically in the .20s and .30s (Miller, 1988). In trying to define the relationship between parents' academic beliefs and their hothousing actions, there is a great deal that is, as yet, not explained.

Some parents who favor hothousing in theory may modify their actions because of characteristics of their child. Birth status (Eaton, Chipperfield, and Singbeil, 1989), gender (McGillicuddy-DeLisi, 1988; Richman, 1990), and children's temperament or special needs (Pelligrini, Brody, and Sigel, 1985) may elicit more directive, controlling behavior from parents.

It would be very useful to study the interrelationship of hothousing plans, actions, and feelings across other samples of parents, including a wider range of socioeconomic and ethnic backgrounds. The mothers in the Academic Environments study had access to far greater resources than do most parents, whether they chose to build a hothouse or not. To return to an earlier metaphor, it is easier to be effective general contractors when parents have the "social capital" to consult with experts, to engage capable assistants, and to consider many options for implementing their plans.

References

Bronfenbrenner, U. *The Ecology of Human Development*. Cambridge, Mass.: Harvard University Press, 1979.

Eaton, W. O., Chipperfield, J. G., and Singbeil, C. E. "Birth Order and Activity Level in Children." *Developmental Psychology*, 1989, *25*, 668–672.

Erikson, E. H. *Childhood and Society*. New York: Norton, 1950.

Hyson, M. C., and Hirsh-Pasek, K. "Academic Environments in Early Childhood: Challenge or Pressure?" Unpublished final report to the Spencer Foundation, Chicago, 1989.

Hyson, M. C., Hirsh-Pasek, K., Rescorla, L., Cone, J., and Martell-Boinske, L. "Ingredients of Parental 'Pressure' in Early Childhood." *Journal of Applied Developmental Psychology*, in press.

Maccoby, E. E., and Martin, J. "Socialization in the Context of the Family." In P. Mussen (ed.), *Handbook of Child Psychology*. Vol. 3. (4th ed.) New York: Wiley, 1983.

McGillicuddy-DeLisi, A. V. "Sex Differences in Parental Teaching Behaviors." *Merrill-Palmer Quarterly*, 1988, *34*, 147–162.

Miller, S. A. "Parents' Beliefs About Children's Cognitive Development." *Child Development*, 1988, *59*, 259–285.

Minuchin, P. *The Middle Years of Childhood*. Monterey, Calif.: Brooks/Cole, 1977.

Pelligrini, A. D., Brody, G. H., and Sigel, I. E. "Parents' Teaching Strategies with Their Children: The Effects of Parental and Child Status Variables." *Journal of Psycholinguistic Research*, 1985, *14*, 509–521.

Pratt, M. W., Kerig, P., Cowan, P. A., and Cowan, C. P. "Mothers and Fathers Teaching 3-Year-Olds: Authoritative Parenting and Adult Scaffolding of Young Children's Learning." *Developmental Psychology*, 1988, *24*, 832–839.

Richman, B. "Parental Achievement Expectations and Parental Warmth: Their Relationship to Development in Young Children." Unpublished doctoral dissertation, Department of Human Development, Bryn Mawr College, 1990.

Segal, M. "A Study of Maternal Beliefs and Values Within the Context of an Intervention Program." In I. E. Sigel (ed.), *Parental Belief Systems: The Psychological Consequences for Children*. Hillsdale, N.J.: Erlbaum, 1985.

Sigel, I. E., and McGillicuddy-DeLisi, A. V. "Parents as Teachers of Their Children: A Distancing Behavior Model." In A. D. Pelligrini and T. D. Yawkey (eds.), *The Development of Oral and Written Language in Social Contexts*. Norwood, N.J.: Ablex, 1984.

Skinner, E. A. "Determinants of Mother-Sensitive and Contingent-Responsive Behavior: The Role of Childrearing Beliefs and Socioeconomic Status." In I. E. Sigel (ed.), *Parental Belief Systems: The Psychological Consequences for Children*. Hillsdale, N.J.: Erlbaum, 1985.

Valsiner, J. *Culture and the Development of Children's Action*. New York: Wiley, 1987.

Vygotsky, L. S. *Mind in Society: The Development of Higher Psychological Processes*. Cambridge, Mass.: Harvard University Press, 1978.

Wertsch, J. *Vygotsky and the Social Formation of Mind*. Cambridge, Mass.: Harvard University Press, 1985.

Marion C. Hyson is associate professor in the Department of Individual and Family Studies, University of Delaware, Newark, specializing in early childhood education and early emotional development.

Highly academic environments have little benefit for children's academic skills, may dampen creative expression, and may create some anxiety. These effects, however, are less dramatic than some have claimed.

Pressure or Challenge in Preschool? How Academic Environments Affect Children

Kathy Hirsh-Pasek

Bloom (1964) writes that over 50 percent of adult intelligence is acquired by the age of four years. Assuming a causal relationship between this early knowledge and later intellectual ability, many argue that we should fill young minds full of information so that we can increase the intelligence of our children and can groom the next generation of leaders. Indeed, the past two decades of infancy research support this contention insofar as the work has revealed the striking abilities that infants and young toddlers have to process and learn new information.

This line of reasoning represents the extreme position taken by those who endorse proposals for early academic orientations during the preschool years (Doman, 1964, 1979, 1984; Eastman and Barr, 1985; Engelmann and Engelmann, 1981; see Storfer, 1990, for a review). Academic attitudes and practices in the early years, they suggest, provide a challenge that enhances young minds and increases academic and intellectual abilities. By this account, both advantaged and disadvantaged children should benefit from this intellectual "head start."

In direct opposition to this position are outspoken developmental psychologists and educators (Elkind, 1981, 1987; Sigel, 1987; Gallagher and Coche, 1987; Kagan and Zigler, 1987; Bredekamp, 1987) who argue that highly academic expectations and practices may harm young children by compromising normal development. Academic orientations for preschoolers, they suggest, offer "too much too soon" and constitute pressures that could result in social and emotional problems.

At the core of this debate on the role of early academics for preschoolers is the question of child outcomes. How do academic orientations in the home and school affect the development of our children? This chapter directly investigates this question by exploring relationships between the diverse philosophies and practices evidenced in the home and school (see Rescorla, this volume [Chapter Two]; Hyson, this volume [Chapters Three and Four]; and subsequent academic, social, emotional, and creative development. Thus, in this final chapter on the Academic Environments project, I go beyond the rhetoric of the debate on child outcomes and ask the empirical question of whether academic orientations in the preschool serve as a challenge or as a pressure to children.

There is not, to my knowledge, any research that deals explicitly with this question. Yet, a number of research projects indirectly bear on the issue. For example, findings from several studies point to a correlation between parents' expectations about academic achievement and actual academic achievement. Often, these parental expectations and concerns about academic progress are expressed through child-rearing patterns that reinforce academic achievement in the children (Miller, 1988; Sigel and McGillicuddy-DeLisi, 1984; Entwisle and Hayduk, 1982). Sigel (1982) and his colleagues demonstrated that environments that encourage more verbal interaction and that are more developmentally appropriate seem to increase cognitive and social skills in children. Hess and McDevitt (1984) found that mothers who used indirect control teaching techniques rather than more didactic approaches tended to have children who were more academically proficient. Finally, Hess, Holloway, Price, and Dickson (1982) suggested that parental concern over school was positively related to school progress and reading achievement in elementary school. Collectively, these findings suggest that early academic environments foster academic success if the academics are delivered in a warm, developmentally appropriate atmosphere.

While some investigators have examined links between academic attitudes and practices and academic skills, research on how these academic environments affect social, emotional, or creative development is scant. There is research that suggests a relationship between academic achievement and social status (Green, Forehand, Beck, and Vosk, 1980; Hartup, 1989), in that smarter children are often more popular. However, these studies were not performed with preschool-aged children. Furthermore, none of the research reported above focused on how academic attitudes and practices in both home and school affect development more globally.

The research reported here, in contrast, viewed parental attitudes and behaviors and school philosophy and practices as predictor variables for child outcomes in three areas: academic achievement, creativity, and emotional well-being. The research used a subset of measures from the larger Academic Environments study. A more complete presentation of these measures and results is in Hirsh-Pasek, Hyson, and Rescorla (1990).

The Children Studied

The subjects for this study were ninety four-to-five-year-old prekindergarten children and their mothers. Fifty-six of the children were followed and investigated at the end of their kindergarten year. This follow-up sample was selected to reflect the full range of characteristics of the larger sample. As described in the Editors' Notes of this volume, all of the families in our study lived in relatively affluent metropolitan areas; the children attended preschools varying widely in teaching philosophy, from academic, teacher-directed instruction to more play-oriented, child-centered programs.

Measures

The aim of this research was to determine how predictor variables from the home and school affected selected areas of child development. Predictor measures allowed the evaluation of parental attitudes and behaviors and of school philosophies and practices. Child outcome measures involved the assessment of academic skills and cognitive ability, creativity, and emotional well-being.

Predictor Measures. The measures of family and school characteristics used in this study are discussed in greater detail in Chapters Two, Three, and Four of this volume. They included measures of *parental attitude* with the Educational Attitude Scale (EAS) (Rescorla, Hyson, Hirsh-Pasek, and Cone, 1990; Rescorla, this volume [Chapter Two]) and the Developmental Expectations Card Sort (Hess, Price, Dickson, and Conroy, 1981) and of *parental behavior* in the Etch-a-Sketch and sticker pictures tasks (Hyson, Hirsh-Pasek, Rescorla, Cone, and Martell-Boinske, in press; Hyson, this volume [Chapter Three]). They also included measures of *school philosophy* as measured by the teacher version of the EAS and *school practices* as assessed by the Classroom Practices Inventory (Hyson, Hirsh-Pasek, Rescorla, Cone, and Martell-Boinske, in press; Hyson, this volume [Chapter Four]). These measures in hand, my colleagues and I could begin to ask how they related to child outcome.

Child Outcome Measures. We chose child outcome measures that allowed us to evaluate the children in areas of academic performance, creativity, and emotional well-being.

Academic Outcome Measures. Three measures were employed to assess academic outcomes. First, we used the Academic Skills Inventory (preschool academic skills test), designed for children four to six years of age, to assess the acquisition of skills such as letter, word, and number recognition and shape and color naming (Boehm and Slater, 1981). Second, we used the PASS (Program for Auxiliary Services to Schools) Kindergarten Academic Skills Test, a slightly modified version of the PASS First-Grade Screening Test described by Whiteman (1987). Items on the test tap letter and number recognition, visual discrimination, and number concepts. Third, we used the Coloured Progressive Matrices (Raven, Court, and Raven, 1984) to assess logical reasoning and problem-solving skills independently of academic knowledge.

Creativity. To assess creativity, we employed the Torrance Test of Preschool Creative Thinking (Torrance, 1983), in which children are asked to perform certain actions or to describe a series of actions. For example, they are asked to move between two lines or to throw away a paper cup in as many different ways as they can imagine. Creativity was assessed by the originality of the child's responses.

Emotional Well-Being. Finally, emotional well-being was assessed in three ways. First, *perceived competence* was examined with Harter and Pike's (1984) Pictorial Scale of Perceived Competence and Social Acceptance for Young Children, which measures the child's perception of his or her own competence and his or her acceptance by others. Second, after the child participated in several of the tests, *performance anxiety* was rated by the experimenters on a scale ranging from "very nervous, fearful" to "very relaxed." Third, the children were asked about their *attitudes toward school* in a test called the Measurement of Young Children's Attitudes Toward School (MYCATS). Developed for the present study by Van Trieste (1989), MYCATS tapped children's general feelings toward school, their perceptions of their teachers, and their perceived difficulty with or enjoyment of school activities.

Results

As described in Chapters Two, Three, and Four of this volume, parents and schools in the Academic Environments study varied widely in beliefs and practices regarding early academic exposure. Some parents and schools encouraged the mastery of early academic skills, while others were less didactic and more child-oriented. Furthermore, parents who were more academically inclined tended to behave in ways consistent with their philosophy and to send their children to schools that shared the same philosophy. Given this variability and relative consistency in the predictor measures, we were interested in how well these attitudinal and behavioral variables predicted child outcomes.

Using a number of different analyses, we examined relationships between the school and home variables and academic, creative, and social/emotional development. Correlational analyses were the most informative. Turning to academic outcomes, for example, we found that maternal academic expectations had a positive, but short-lived, association with academic skill. In preschool, but not in kindergarten, higher maternal expectations were associated with an increase in academic skills. Highly academic preschool environments, however, had no effect on academic skills within this sample. Neither maternal attitudes nor maternal and school practices predicted ability on the Raven's test of reasoning. Thus, it appears that young children can learn what they are taught about numbers and letters, but that the advantage of learning this material at an early age all but dissipates by kindergarten, when the other children catch up. Further, this early learning of numbers and letters had no noticeable impact on logical reasoning, as children from both more academic and less academic environments fared equally on the Raven's measure. Focusing on the correlations between our predictors and child creativity, we found that mothers who had higher academic expectations, who were more controlling, and who sent their children to more academically oriented schools had children who were slightly less creative than the children of mothers who provided a less academic orientation.

In our final set of correlations, which examined emotional well-being, we found, overall, that the children in our sample thought highly of their own abilities. In preschool, though not in kindergarten, some of these evaluations were related to maternal academic expectations. That is, preschool children whose mothers encouraged academics had a more positive view of their own competence, especially their cognitive competence, relative to peers from less academically oriented families. While there was some detectable relationship, however, it was not only small but also very difficult to interpret. Do children with better skills have better self-images? Do those with more positive perceptions of their own competence tend to work harder and learn better? Whatever the causal relationship turns out to be, the association between self-perception of competence and higher parental expectations was a limited one that was nonexistent by the end of kindergarten.

Although there was some tendency for preschoolers of "high-expectation" mothers to give slightly higher ratings of their own competence, they also demonstrated more performance anxiety during our kindergarten tasks and had a tendency to think less positively about school by the time they reached the end of kindergarten. Perhaps children who think highly of their abilities have a greater fear of failing. However, these findings of high anxiety and of less positive attitudes toward school must be interpreted with caution. The statistical effects were very modest, with only a small proportion of the variance in these measures being attributable to family or school factors. Furthermore, none of the children in our sample, including the kindergarten children from highly academic environments, was intensely anxious, nor was any child intensely negative about school.

One last analysis of interest was not correlational, but comparative. Although most high-expectation parents sent their children to academic preschools, a small number sent their children to more relaxed, play-oriented schools. (It is noteworthy that we were unable to find the reverse: Almost no low-academic parents sent their children to highly academic preschools.) Thus, we could make a comparison between two types of parents with high academic expectations: those who sent their children to high- versus low-academic school environments. Indeed, a comparison of child outcomes from these two groups provides a glimpse of how different academic settings, namely, home and school, can jointly contribute to the child's development. Our parent interviews suggested that some high-expectation mothers recognized their tendency to push their children and wanted to temper their high-expectation home environments with low-academic school settings. The evidence suggests that this strategy may be successful, with the school environment buffering some of the negative effects that arise from academic pressure at home. In our subsample, children of high-academic parents who attended low-academic preschools were at no academic disadvantage. More positively, they showed significantly less test anxiety in preschool and kindergarten and exhibited more positive attitudes toward school than did children whose parents had similar beliefs but who attended academically oriented preschools. This analysis suggests that academic pressure or challenge is not likely to come from a single source but rather from the combination of academic environments that interactively influence each child.

Discussion

One of the goals of this project was to determine whether academic acceleration provided challenge or pressure for young children. The modest correlations that we found permit only tentative answers to this question. Indeed, two interpretations of our data are possible. Under a more conservative interpretation of the data, academic orientations make no difference at all to the child. We have seen that there were no lasting academic advantages for those who received early academic training, and one might argue that differences of relatively low magnitude in creativity and emotional well-being (as were characteristic in our data) are insignificant. That is, in our sample virtually no children could be characterized as extremely anxious. All were fairly creative, and all had fairly positive attitudes toward school. The conservative interpretation of the data, therefore, does not rule in favor of either challenge or pressure.

A second and more liberal interpretation of our data, however, holds that academic orientations provide no advantage to children's scholastic or intellectual development, but that they *do* have negative, albeit modest, consequences for other areas of the child's development. In the correlational analyses, higher academic orientations were related to less creativity, higher levels of test anxiety, and less positive attitudes toward school.

Whichever interpretation is adopted, the results point to a single resolution: If early academic orientations offer no clear benefit to children's development and if they *can* hinder development, there is not a defensible reason to encourage the introduction of formal academic instruction and adult-focused learning during the preschool years. Our findings and those of other studies (see, for example, Schweinhart, Weikart, and Larner, 1986; Hohmann, Banet, and Weikart, 1979; Rawl and O'Tuel, 1982) suggest that both middle-class and disadvantaged children may experience early academic and didactic orientations as more of a pressure than a challenge. Given these findings, it is prudent to let children explore the world at their own pace and to structure educational environments that are child-centered, developmentally appropriate, and maybe even fun.

References

Bloom, P. *Stability and Change in Human Characteristics.* New York: Wiley, 1964.

Boehm, A. E., and Slater, B. R. *Cognitive Skills Assessment Battery.* (2nd ed.) New York: Teachers College Press, 1981.

Bredekamp, S. E. (ed.). *Developmentally Appropriate Practice in Early Childhood Programs Serving Children from Birth Through Age 8.* Washington, D.C.: National Association for the Education of Young Children, 1987.

Doman, G. J. *How to Teach Your Baby to Read.* New York: Random House, 1964.

Doman, G. J. *Teach Your Baby Math.* New York: Simon & Schuster, 1979.

Doman, G. J. *How to Multiply Your Baby's Intelligence.* Garden City, N.Y.: Doubleday, 1984.

Eastman, P., and Barr, J. L. *Your Child Is Smarter than You Think.* London: Jonathan Cape, 1985.

Elkind, D. *The Hurried Child.* Reading, Mass.: Addison-Wesley, 1981.

Elkind, D. *Miseducation: Preschoolers at Risk.* New York: Knopf, 1987.

Engelmann, S., and Engelmann, T. *Give Your Child a Superior Mind.* New York: Cornerstone, 1981.

Entwisle, D., and Hayduk, L. A. *Early Schooling: Cognitive and Affective Outcomes.* Baltimore, Md.: Johns Hopkins University Press, 1982.

Gallagher, J. M., and Coche, J. "Hothousing: The Clinical and Educational Concerns over Pressuring Young Children." *Early Childhood Research Quarterly,* 1987, 2 (3), 203–210.

Green, K. D., Forehand, R., Beck, S. J., and Vosk, B. "An Assessment of the Relationship Among Measures of Children's Social Competence and Children's Academic Achievement." *Child Development,* 1980, 51, 1140–1156.

Harter, S., and Pike, R. "The Pictorial Scale of Perceived Competence and Social Acceptance for Young Children." *Child Development,* 1984, 55, 1969–1982.

Hartup, W. "Social Relationships and Their Developmental Significance." *American Psychologist,* 1989, 44, 120–126.

Hess, R. D., Holloway, S., Price, G., and Dickson, W. P. "Family Environments and the Acquisition of Reading Skills: Towards a More Precise Analysis." In L. M. Laosa and I. E. Sigel (eds.), *Families as Learning Environments for Children.* New York: Plenum, 1982.

Hess, R. D., and McDevitt, T. M. "Some Cognitive Consequences of Maternal Intervention Techniques: A Longitudinal Study." *Child Development,* 1984, 55, 689–703.

Hess, R. D., Price, G. G., Dickson, W. P., and Conroy, M. "Different Roles for Mothers and Teachers: Contrasting Styles of Child Care." In S. Kilmer (ed.), *Advances in Early Education and Day Care.* Vol. 2. Greenwich, Conn.: JAI, 1981.

Hirsh-Pasek, K., Hyson, M. C., and Rescorla, L. "Academic Environments in Preschool: Do They Pressure or Challenge Young Children?" *Early Education and
Development,* 1990, *1* (6), 401–423.

Hohmann, M., Banet, B., and Weikart, D. P. *Young Children in Action: A Manual for
Preschool Educators.* Ypsilanti, Mich.: High/Scope Press, 1979.

Hyson, M. C., Hirsh-Pasek, K., and Rescorla, L. "The Classroom Practices Inventory:
An Observational Instrument Based on NAEYC's Guidelines for Developmentally
Appropriate Practices for 4- and 5-Year-Old Children." *Early Childhood Research
Quarterly,* 1990, *5,* 475–494.

Hyson, M. C., Hirsh-Pasek, K., Rescorla, L., Cone, J., and Martell-Boinske, L. "Ingredients of Parental 'Pressure' in Early Childhood." *Journal of Applied Developmental
Psychology,* in press.

Kagan, S. L., and Zigler, E. F. (eds.). *Early Schooling: The National Debate.* New
Haven, Conn.: Yale University Press, 1987.

Miller, S. A. "Parents' Beliefs About Children's Cognitive Development." *Child Development,* 1988, *59,* 259–285.

Raven, J. C., Court, H. H., and Raven, J. *Coloured Progressive Matrices.* London: H. K.
Lewis, 1984.

Rawl, R. K., and O'Tuel, F. S. "A Comparison of Three Prereading Approaches for
Kindergarten Students." *Reading Improvement,* 1982, *19* (3), 205–211.

Rescorla, L., Hyson, M. C., Hirsh-Pasek, K., and Cone, J. "Academic Expectations
in Mothers of Preschool Children: A Psychometric Study of the Educational
Attitude Scale." *Early Education and Development,* 1990, *1,* 165–184.

Schweinhart, L. J., Weikart, D. P., and Larner, M. B. "Consequences of Three Preschool Curriculum Models Through Age 15." *Early Childhood Research Quarterly,*
1986, *1,* 15–45.

Sigel, I. E. "The Relationship Between Parental Distancing Strategies and the Child's
Cognitive Behavior." In L. M. Laosa and I. E. Sigel (eds.), *Families as Learning
Environments for Children.* New York: Plenum, 1982.

Sigel, I. E. "Does Hothousing Rob Children of Their Childhood?" *Early Childhood
Research Quarterly,* 1987, *2,* 211–225.

Sigel, I. E., and McGillicuddy-DeLisi, A. V. "Parents as Teachers of Their Children:
A Distancing Behavior Model." In A. D. Pelligrini and T. D. Yawkey (eds.), *The
Development of Oral and Written Language in Social Contexts.* Norwood, N.J.: Ablex,
1984.

Storfer, M. D. *Intelligence and Giftedness: The Contributions of Heredity and Early Environment.* San Francisco: Jossey-Bass, 1990.

Torrance, E. P. "Preschool Creativity." In K. D. Paget and B. A. Bracken (eds.), *The
Psychoeducational Assessment of Preschool Children.* Orlando, Fla.: Grune & Stratton,
1983.

Van Trieste, K.M.L. "Academic Environments in Early Childhood: Effects on Young
Children's Self-Perceptions of Competence and Attitudes Toward School." Unpublished master's thesis, Department of Individual and Family Studies, University
of Delaware, 1989.

Whiteman, T. A. "The PASS First-Grade Screening Test: Statistical Analysis and
Predictive Validity." Unpublished manuscript, Department of Human Development, Bryn Mawr College, 1987.

*Kathy Hirsh-Pasek is associate professor in the Department of Psychology, Temple
University, Philadelphia, specializing in areas of language development, reading
acquisition, and early cognitive processes.*

A study of sixty-two preschool and kindergarten programs reveals strong associations between the nature of instruction and the social context.

Characterizing Early Childhood Education Programs

Deborah Stipek

Psychologists have long debated the relative merits of different instructional approaches for young children. The controversy has never been entirely theoretical. But as policymakers return to early childhood education as a means of preventing educational disadvantages of poor children, and as the federal and state governments and local school districts allocate greater resources to early childhood education programs, there is a new urgency to identifying the most effective instructional strategies.

Teacher-Directed Versus Child-Centered Education

The debate on appropriate preschool education typically contrasts a teacher-directed, didactic approach in which the acquisition of basic skills is stressed with a more child-centered approach in which social-emotional development and problem-solving abilities are emphasized. The former is associated with learning theory and is exemplified by Bereiter and Engelmann's (1966) Distar program; the latter is associated with constructivist theories of development and is represented by the British infant school, Montessori, and other programs based on Piagetian principles.

Recent evidence suggests a trend toward didactic teaching practices and away from child-centered approaches (Durkin, 1987; Hiebert, 1988; Spodek, 1982). This shift is presumably occurring, in part, because of widespread concerns about student achievement. However, many child devel-

The research described in this chapter was conducted with Denise Daniels, Darlene Galluzzo, and Sharon Milburn. It was supported by the Smith Richardson Foundation.

opment experts have warned that the short-term gains in achievement that didactic programs produce could come at the expense of positive social-motivational development and long-term achievement gains. Experts have argued, for example, that didactic, teacher-controlled instruction undermines young children's intrinsic interest in learning (Katz, 1987), their perceptions of competence (Kamii, 1985), and their willingness to take academic risks (Elkind, 1987), and that it fosters dependency on adult authority for defining tasks and evaluating outcomes (Elkind, 1986).

Research on Program Effects

Consistent with experts' claims, a few studies suggest that the short-term positive effects on achievement of structured, didactic preschool programs may, in the long term, cost some children their self-confidence and pleasure in learning and ultimately undermine achievement gains. For example, Schweinhart, Weikart, and Larner (1986) found that poor children who had participated in a Distar preschool program were more likely to claim that their family felt poorly about how they were doing, and they were less likely to read books at age fifteen than were children who had been in more child-centered preschool programs. Miller and Bizzell (1983) report that boys who received teacher-directed, didactic preschool instruction gained the most in IQ initially, but by eighth grade they had considerably lower achievement scores than did boys who had been in nondidactic programs. The relative decline among boys in didactic programs might have been caused, in part, by negative social-motivational effects.

However, these studies are only suggestive. Criticism of recent trends toward more teacher-directed instruction has been based primarily on theory and evidence from studies of older children. The validity of experts' predictions has not been tested in early childhood programs, and the debate remains primarily rhetorical.

In order to study social-motivational as well as academic achievement effects of different program approaches, it is important to examine the instructional practices of programs. Classroom research on older children has demonstrated that *how* a curriculum is implemented is as important as the content of the curriculum. For example, emphasis on performance, external evaluation, and social comparisons has been shown to result in low self-confidence and cautiousness, especially in children who perform poorly compared to their classmates. Both lack of individualization and restriction of child choice have been shown to undermine children's intrinsic interest in school tasks (see Stipek, 1988, for a review of this literature).

Alternatives to the Dichotomy

Some of the classroom variables, such as individualization and child choice, that affect social-motivational and achievement outcomes are often included in the distinctions made between child-centered and didactic approaches to early childhood education. However, observations of existing programs might reveal a more complicated picture than the child-centered versus didactic instruction dichotomy suggests. For example, teacher-directed instruction associated with the didactic approach could be conducted by a teacher who is punitive and humiliates children publicly for their mistakes, or by a supportive, nurturing teacher who emphasizes learning over correctness. In the former but not the latter case, instruction is likely to have negative effects on children's self-confidence and willingness to participate. Child choice associated with child-centered approaches is presumed to foster intrinsic interest and learning. But choice would not have these positive effects if products are compared and criticized so that children become afraid to select challenging tasks that can help them advance their skills and understanding. If such combinations exist, we need a more differentiated way to characterize early childhood education programs.

A few researchers have suggested alternatives to the teacher-directed versus child-centered dichotomy described above. Lay-Dopyera and Dopyera (1990), for example, differentiate between two child-centered curricula: one in which there is very little prestructuring and limiting of children's choices and another in which teachers prepare activities and limit child choices on the basis of their knowledge of their children's interests and competencies. This is a useful distinction, with the second type of program representing a middle ground between didactic and child-centered approaches. Schweinhart, Weikart, and Larner (1986) suggest a two-by-two categorization, with the role of the teacher as either initiator or responder being one factor and the role of the child as either initiator or responder being the other factor. The category defined by teacher-as-initiator and child-as-responder includes didactic programs, such as Distar. Child-as-initiator and teacher-as-responder programs include child-centered programs. Schweinhart, Weikart, and Larner include High/Scope among programs in which both child and teacher are the initiators; they refer to programs in which neither child or teacher are initiators as "custodial."

These attempts to differentiate preschool programs are helpful. But the characterizations do not incorporate aspects of instructional practice and elements of the social context known to affect social-motivational development, and we do not know to what degree they represent programs in the real world.

Research Goals

The research reported here was an attempt to create an empirically based approach to differentiating early childhood education programs with regard to a broad array of instructional practices. The goals were to identify conceptually meaningful dimensions on which a large and diverse group of early childhood education programs varied and, on the basis of these dimensions, to create a typology of programs that reflects the way instructional practices cohere in the real world.

Program Selection. My colleagues and I observed and categorized sixty-two preschool and kindergarten classrooms in the greater Los Angeles area. Programs were selected on the basis of reputation and conversations with directors, principals, and teachers to ensure a good distribution in terms of the curricula, the ethnic and social classes of the children served, and the types of program (for example, public versus private). A few of the programs were based on nationally recognized approaches (for example, High/Scope, Montessori). Twenty-three of the programs served primarily poor children (over 70 percent), thirty-five programs served primarily middle-class children, and the remaining four programs served a heterogeneous population with respect to social class. Students were predominantly white (over 70 percent) in eighteen of the programs, African-American in eight, Latino in fifteen, and Asian in two. The remaining nineteen programs served an ethnically mixed population. One program was a Head Start center, thirty-one were private, and thirty were in public school districts. Among the private programs, twelve were affiliated with a church or synagogue and thirteen were for-profit. We cannot be sure that the sample is truly representative of existing preschools and kindergartens in the United States or even in Los Angeles, but it is very diverse.

Observation Protocol. The development of the observation protocol was guided by our interest in social-motivational and academic achievement effects of educational programs on young children. Because almost no research has assessed the social-motivational effects of instructional practices in early childhood education programs, prior research conducted on older children and adults was used to determine which aspects of instruction and classroom organization to code.

The observation protocol developed for this study was complex. Observers, who spent one full day in each program, made twenty-seven judgments about *each* organized (teacher-planned) activity. Some of the judgments concerned the nature of the activity (for example, intellectual, artistic, motor; paper-and-pencil, manipulatives, discussion), and others concerned how the activity was implemented (for example, whether children were allowed or encouraged to work with peers, whether they were required to finish the task, how much discretion children had in carrying out the teacher's instructions, whether the teacher emphasized correctness, enjoyment, or learning, if and how the outcomes were evaluated). In addition to these descriptions of teacher-planned activities, thirty-six summary judgments were made at the end of the day. For example, judgments were made about each teacher's warmth and responsiveness, the diversity of activities, whether playtime and work time were clearly differentiated, and how frequently rewards were given and social comparisons made. Finally, observational ratings were supplemented by teachers' responses to several interview questions (such as on homework practices). All items involved a 3- or 4-point scale, which, for most items, involved descriptive alternatives. For example, for the item concerning choice in playmates and work mates, the alternatives were (1) "teacher determines whom children work/play with," (2) "children have some discretion, limited by teacher grouping or direction," and (3) "children decide whom to work/play with; teacher may suggest." The item was scored 1, 2, or 3, depending on whether the observer selected the first, second, or third option, respectively.

Analyses and Results

The variables in the observation protocol were first grouped into six subscales reflecting program orientation and emphasis. Relationships among these subscale data were analyzed using factor analysis. Cluster analysis was then used to classify the sixty-two early childhood programs in terms of these six dimensions.

Grouping of Variables. Because the large number of variables precluded use of factor analysis, variables were grouped using an analytic strategy that was guided both by an a priori conceptual framework and by intercorrelations observed among the variables. Thus, variables that were related conceptually were grouped if they were also strongly and significantly correlated with each other. Some variables were dropped because there was too little variance or because they were not significantly associated with any other variables. In a few cases, conceptually different groupings were combined because several sets of variables were closely associated statistically. For example, a set of variables related to the amount of choice available to the children (such as in selecting activities and work mates) was strongly correlated with sets of variables related to the diversity of activities and materials available and the amount of social interaction and peer assistance allowed or encouraged. Although conceptual distinctions among these sets of variables were useful, the variables were associated so strongly with each other statistically that separate subscales were not justified.

This analytic process yielded six subscales that differentiated classrooms, with each subscale composed of five to eleven items. Programs with high scores on the *child initiative* subscale (coefficient alphas for preschools and kindergartens were .88 and .89, respectively) gave children more choice in activities, offered more diverse activities and materials in a play-like (as opposed to businesslike) atmosphere, and encouraged more social interaction than did programs with low scores. This subscale is closely related to descriptions of child-centered programs based on constructivist theories of child development. Programs with high scores on the *teacher warmth* subscale (alphas = .95 and .91 for preschools and kindergartens, respectively) had teachers who were nurturing, accepting, respectful, and responsive to children. Programs scoring high on the *positive control* subscale (alphas = .83 and .79) were characterized by positive approaches to maintaining student engagement in sanctioned activities and minimizing misbehavior (for example, clear instructions, novel, interesting activities, without ridicule, threats, or punishment to motivate children).

In programs scoring high on the *academic emphasis* subscale (alphas = .78 and .83), subject matter was clearly differentiated and children spent a relatively large amount of time focused on academic topics, frequently using commercially prepared materials (such as worksheets). Tasks were often closed-ended (only one right answer) and were usually not embedded in practical or personally meaningful activities. Teachers in kindergartens with high scores on this subscale frequently gave flashcards or worksheets for homework. In programs high on the *performance pressure* subscale (alphas = .81 and .76) teachers were relatively more likely to give negative evaluations and criticize wrong responses, and to use threats and punishment to motivate children. They were also more likely to emphasize outcomes of tasks and less likely to emphasize enjoyment or learning or to tolerate nonconventional (but nondisruptive) behavior. In programs scoring high on the *evaluation stress* subscale (alphas = .81 and .78), external evaluation and rewards were given relatively more frequently and social comparison was emphasized.

The groupings for the preschool and kindergarten classrooms were the same, with only a few exceptions. For example, flashcards and worksheets were given as homework in some kindergartens but almost no preschools. Consequently, this variable was included on the academic emphasis subscale for kindergarten, but not for preschool programs.

Factor Analyses of Subscales. These six subscales were not independent. Nonorthogonal factor analyses of the six subscales resulted in a single factor, which accounted for 67 percent of the variance for preschools and 58 percent of the variance for kindergarten classrooms. Factor loadings ranged from .53 to -.96, with a mean of .79. The first three subscores (child initiative, teacher warmth, and positive control)—henceforth referred to as "social context" subscales—loaded positively on the factor; the second three subscores (academic emphasis, performance pressure, and evaluation stress)—henceforth referred to as "teacher-directed instruction" subscales—loaded negatively on the factor. Thus, programs that had relatively high scores on the social context subscales had relatively low scores on the teacher-directed instruction subscales, and vice versa.

The analyses, therefore, suggest a unidimensional characterization of early childhood education programs. The poles of this continuum are consistent with the distinction that early childhood education experts often make between child-centered programs and teacher-directed, didactic programs.

Clusters of Programs. This unidimensional picture was supported by the results of the two cluster analyses done (one for preschools and one for kindergartens) to create groups of programs that were similar to each other with regard to the six dimensions assessed. The first cluster, which we refer to as "child-centered," included programs that were very high on the three social context subscales and very low on the three teacher-directed instruction subscales. Twelve kindergarten and ten preschool classrooms fell into this cluster. A second cluster, which we labeled "didactic," contained ten kindergarten and nine preschool classrooms and included programs that were high on the teacher-directed instruction subscales and low on the social context subscales. The third cluster, designated as "intermediate," contained thirteen kindergartens and eight preschools and fell somewhere in between these two extremes; these programs were intermediate in terms of both the social context and teacher-directed instruction subscales.

Combinations *Not* Observed. What is most striking about these results is the absence of some combinations of instructional practices. For example, out of twenty-four preschool and kindergarten programs that were high (in the top third of the distribution) on the combined teacher-directed instruction subscales, *none* was also high (in the top third of the distribution), and only seven were intermediate, on the combined social-climate subscales. Does an emphasis on academic achievement and teacher-directed instruction preclude a positive social context?

To some degree the negative relationship found between these two sets of variables was predictable. For example, it would be difficult to maintain a playlike atmosphere while emphasizing correct outcomes and criticizing incorrect responses. But the observed combinations are not the only combinations possible. There are no logical or practical reasons why teachers cannot emphasize basic skills—even using worksheets—and at the same time be nurturing and responsive, provide children with choices, encourage peer cooperation, and emphasize enjoyment.

Most early childhood experts would not expect highly teacher-directed, didactic instruction in a negative social context to have positive effects on children. It is the child-centered approach, in which performance outcomes and external evaluation are de-emphasized, that is most often promoted in the early childhood education literature. However, an emphasis on basic skills may be inevitable in the current social-political climate of concern about academic achievement. It is, therefore, important to determine why a strong academic emphasis tends to be associated with a negative social climate, and whether negative effects of didactic instruction could be alleviated by a positive social context.

"Intermediate" Approaches. An important finding of this research is that all programs did not cluster at the extremes. To the contrary, the programs observed in this study were fully distributed along the continuum.

Thus, many of the programs observed were intermediate in terms of both social context and academic emphasis. What is not clear at this point is whether children benefit more from an intermediate level of teacher-directed instruction in a moderately positive social context, or from an extremely positive social context in which teacher-directed instructional approaches are not used at all. It is possible that some children benefit more from one type of context and other children benefit more from the other. The effects of this intermediate approach are worth studying because it may have more positive effects on children's learning and social-motivational development than a highly teacher-directed approach. An intermediate level of teacher-directed instruction coupled with a moderately positive social context should also satisfy policymakers' and parents' concerns about academic achievement.

Conclusion

Early childhood education experts have made many claims about appropriate instructional practices for young children. These claims are often based on sound theory and research, but many claims have not been systematically tested. Research on the effects of different instructional approaches to child motivation and learning is essential, particularly given the high levels of participation of American children in preschool and kindergarten programs and the current emphasis on early childhood education as a means to redress educational problems of poor, minority children. If we devote scarce resources to such programs, we should be confident that we are providing an educational experience that enhances young children's social-motivational and intellectual development.

References

Bereiter, C., and Engelmann, S. *Teaching Disadvantaged Children in the Preschool.* Englewood Cliffs, N.J.: Prentice-Hall, 1966.

Durkin, D. "A Classroom-Observation Study of Reading Instruction in Kindergarten." *Early Childhood Research Quarterly,* 1987, 2 (3), 275–300.

Elkind, D. "Formal Education and Early Childhood Education: An Essential Difference." *Phi Delta Kappan,* 1986, 67 (9), 631–636.

Elkind, D. *Miseducation: Preschoolers at Risk.* New York: Knopf, 1987.

Hiebert, E. "The Role of Literacy Experiences in Early Childhood Programs." *Elementary School Journal,* 1988, 89 (2), 161–171.

Kamii, C. "Leading Primary Education Toward Excellence: Beyond Worksheets and Drill." *Young Children,* 1985, 40 (6), 3–9.

Katz, L. "Early Education: What Should Young Children Be Doing?" In S. L. Kagan and E. F. Zigler (eds.), *Early Schooling: The National Debate.* New Haven, Conn.: Yale University Press, 1987.

Lay-Dopyera, M., and Dopyera, J. "The Child-Centered Curriculum." In C. Seefeldt (ed.), *Continuing Issues in Early Childhood Education.* Westerville, Ohio: Merrill, 1990.

Miller, L. B., and Bizzell, R. P. "Long-Term Effects of Four Preschool Programs: Sixth, Seventh, and Eighth Grades." *Child Development,* 1983, *54* (3), 727–741.

Schweinhart, L. J., Weikart, D. P., and Larner, M. B. "Consequences of Three Preschool Curriculum Models Through Age 15." *Early Childhood Research Quarterly,* 1986, *1* (1), 15–45.

Spodek, B. "The Kindergarten: A Retrospective and Contemporary View." In L. Katz (ed.), *Current Topics in Early Childhood Education.* Vol. 4. Norwood, N.J.: Ablex, 1982.

Stipek, D. *Motivation to Learn: From Theory to Practice.* Englewood Cliffs, N.J.: Prentice-Hall, 1988.

Deborah Stipek is professor of education and head of the Developmental Studies Program at the University of California, Los Angeles.

Disadvantaged children benefit most from high-quality preschool
programs that encourage child-initiated learning.

Disadvantaged Children and Curriculum Effects

David P. Weikart, Lawrence J. Schweinhart

A wide range of social changes and economic pressures have combined to focus the nation's attention on education. The prolonged failure of various educational reform efforts to resolve the achievement problems of black and Hispanic minority youth, the increasingly vicious nature of teenage crime, and the continued presence of widespread drug abuse have all gained increasing public attention. Something must be done to ameliorate these situations. A democracy such as the United States cannot endure without an educated work force.

Within this context of national need, the usefulness of high-quality early childhood education as part of the solution cannot be overemphasized. Various studies have demonstrated the value of disadvantaged children attending such programs in reducing social problems and increasing life chances. Both longitudinal studies, such as those reported by the Consortium for Longitudinal Studies (1983), and overviews of short-term evaluations of National Head Start programs (McKey, Condelli, Ganson, Barrett, McConkey, and Plantz, 1985) indicate the general importance of early childhood education. Among individual studies, the High/Scope Perry Preschool Project found that disadvantaged children who attended a good preschool program, compared to a randomly assigned control group, were significantly more likely to graduate from high school, enroll in postsecondary education, and become employed. They were significantly less likely to be assigned to special education classes, commit crimes, have children as teenagers, or receive general welfare assistance (Berrueta-Clement, Schweinhart, Barnett, Epstein, and Weikart, 1984). Data such as these have filtered into the popular press (Waldman, 1990). Early education can work

NEW DIRECTIONS FOR CHILD DEVELOPMENT, no. 53, Fall 1991 © Jossey-Bass Inc., Publishers

and contribute to the welfare of children, their families, and society at large. While clearly not a panacea, early childhood education is part of the solution to social and economic problems faced by the nation.

However, buried underneath the findings of these early childhood education reports is the fact that the only successful early childhood education programs are those of high quality. There are many studies of typical, run-of-the-mill projects that have not produced much in the way of positive outcomes. For example, McKey and others (1985) reviewed many studies of Head Start programs around the country that reported minimal, if any, positive effects. To illustrate the difficulty of obtaining positive results, one early large-scale project claimed success because children in the preschool service group did not lose as many IQ points as did the "no preschool" group (DiLorenzo, Salter, and Brady, 1969). Even some members of the Consortium for Longitudinal Studies (1983) reported programs with uneven, inconsistent results. Only studies of carefully designed, high-quality programs such as the High/Scope Perry Preschool Project, consistently applied over long periods, have fully indicated the potential of early education.

Various approaches have been proposed to support high-quality programming. The National Association for the Education of Young Children (NAEYC, 1984) has developed perhaps the most elaborate system of evaluation, with commitment to a full range of operational goals for programs. State licensing standards, which are applied, albeit unevenly, in all states (Morgan, 1986), represent a narrower view of acceptable operational goals.

A number of studies have attempted to identify critical elements in program success. A few studies have looked at program operation from the point of view of staffing and group size, such as the National Child Care Staffing study (Whitebook, Howes, and Phillips, 1989) and the National Day Care study (Ruopp, Travers, Glantz, and Coelen, 1979). Only a very few studies have examined the impact of early childhood education in terms of curriculum effects, holding staffing and other operational issues constant (Karnes, Schwedel, and Williams, 1983; Miller and Bizzell, 1983; Schweinhart, Weikart, and Larner, 1986; Weikart, Epstein, Schweinhart, and Bond, 1978). The High/Scope Preschool Curriculum Comparison study, which is discussed in this chapter, was specifically designed to test the impact of various major methods of curriculum and operation. It also is the only study available using random assignment of samples to each possible condition. Long-term follow-up data from the High/Scope project are fully presented in Schweinhart, Weikart, and Larner (1986). We review here the major outcomes from the High/Scope Perry Preschool Project and then discuss their implications for program development for disadvantaged children.

The Curriculum Models

The preschool curriculum models used in the High/Scope Preschool Curriculum Comparison study represent three, theoretically distinct approaches to preschool education. These approaches differ with respect to the degree of initiative expected of the child and of the teacher: whether the child's primary role in the program is to initiate or respond and whether the teacher's primary role is to initiate or respond (Weikart, 1972; Kohlberg and Mayer, 1972).

The *programmed-learning approach* uses the "teacher initiates/child responds" model and is represented by the Direct Instruction preschool program developed by Bereiter and Engelmann (1966). In this approach, classroom activities are prescribed by behavioral sequences of stimuli, responses, and positive reinforcements. Objectives are clearly defined academic skills. The underlying psychological theory is behaviorist.

The *open-framework approach* uses a "teacher initiates/child initiates" model and is represented by the High/Scope curriculum (Hohmann, Banet, and Weikart, 1979). Here, classroom activities revolve around teacher-organized key experiences designed to promote intellectual and social development, as well as child-initiated content that determines what the children undertake. The underlying psychological theory is cognitive-developmental, as exemplified in the work of Jean Piaget.

The *child-centered approach* uses the "teacher responds/child initiates" model and is represented by a nursery school program that incorporates the elements of what has historically constituted good nursery school practice. In these classrooms, activities are the teacher's responses to the child's expressed needs and interests. The teacher encourages children to actively engage in free play. Historically, the underlying psychological theory has been psychoanalytic, as exemplified in the work of Sigmund Freud.

Common Characteristics of the Programs

All three programs in the High/Scope study were part of the same research project, with the same director (Weikart), funding source, personnel policies, and position in the school system. All three programs in the study had two components: classroom sessions (with two teachers and fifteen or sixteen children) and educational home visits. Classroom sessions lasting two and a half hours were held Monday through Friday. A teacher visited each mother and child at home in ninety-minute sessions every two weeks.

Sample Selection and Assignment

Sixty-eight children met the study's criteria for inclusion. They were residents of Ypsilanti, Michigan, became three years old between 1967 and 1969 inclusively, lived in families of low socioeconomic status, and were at risk for school failure according to test scores. Each year, the children in a new wave were randomly assigned to three groups. The three groups were then randomly assigned to the three preschool curriculum models.

Initial Sample and Group Characteristics. Of the sixty-eight children in the program sample, 65 percent were black and 54 percent were female. The families lived in poverty, with one out of three receiving welfare assistance. In the 75 percent of families for whom fathers were present, 98 percent of the fathers and 38 percent of the mothers were employed in unskilled labor. Fathers averaged nine years of schooling, and mothers averaged ten. The average household had 6.7 persons, or one person per room. Curriculum groups were similar on the key characteristics of gender, family socioeconomic status, and child IQ at program entry.

Attrition Through Age Fifteen. Of the sixty-eight youngsters in the initial program sample, fifty-four were interviewed at age fifteen—a retention rate of 79 percent. Comparison of the age-fifteen sample to the original sample indicates that the two samples were virtually equivalent in every respect.

Measurement of Preschool Curriculum Outcomes

The outcome domains measured in the curriculum study included intellectual and scholastic performance over time and self-reports at age fifteen of various aspects of social behavior and attitudes: juvenile delinquency, family relations, social activities, school behavior and attitudes, mental health, employment, and financial affairs.

The children completed several instruments measuring aspects of intellectual performance at various times: the Stanford-Binet (Terman and Merrill, 1970) and the Wechsler Intelligence Scale for Children (Wechsler, 1949), the California Achievement Test (Tiegs and Clark, 1963), and the Adult Performance Level (APL) Survey (American College Testing Program, 1976). The APL is a multiple-choice test developed for students in adult education programs to assess the skills needed for educational and economic success in modern society. It measures application of five skills (identification of facts and terms, reading, writing, computation, and problem solving) to five knowledge areas (community resources, occupational knowledge, consumer economics, health, and government and law).

Juvenile delinquency and other aspects of social behavior were assessed by self-report procedures, which are frequently used by delinquency researchers (for example, Empey, 1978). The juvenile delinquency scale used came from the work of Martin Gold of the Survey Research Center at the University of Michigan's Institute for Social Research (see the Monitoring the Future survey reported by Bachman and Johnston, 1978).

Results

The results are briefly summarized below with respect to intellectual performance, school achievement, and social behavior differences between the three preschool approaches.

Preschool Curriculum Effects on Intellectual Performance. When the mean IQs of the three preschool curriculum groups were examined separately, differences between them were quite small. During the first year of the preschool program, mean IQs rose between 23 and 29 points, moving the groups of children out of the at-risk category. During the second preschool year, mean IQs of the High/Scope and nursery school groups dropped nine to ten points, whereas mean IQ of the Direct Instruction group dropped only three points, thereby achieving the only statistically significant intellectual advantage among groups at any testing. From the end of kindergarten onward, curriculum groups did not differ in mean IQs and stabilized in the range of 90 to 100, a significant and important increase over entry IQs.

Preschool Curriculum Effects on School Achievement. The achievement scores gathered on all the children were from the California Achievement Tests (lower primary form W) at the end of first and second grades. The APL Survey was used at age fifteen. There were no significant differences in mean achievement at any point.

Preschool Curriculum Effects on Social Behavior. Juvenile delinquency and other aspects of social behavior were examined for the curriculum study sample by self-reports at age fifteen. According to these data, the Direct Instruction group engaged in twice as many delinquent acts (thirteen) as did the other two curriculum groups (the nursery group had seven and the High/Scope group had five), including five times as many acts of property violence and twice as many acts of drug abuse and such status offenses as running away from home. Other areas of social behavior corroborated this pattern of relatively poor social performance by the Direct Instruction group: poor family relations, less participation in sports or school job appointments, lower expectations for educational attainment, and less reaching out to others for help with personal problems. For most of these variables, the sharpest contrast was with the High/Scope group, whose social behavior was relatively positive. The curriculum groups performed similarly to each other in the spheres of employment and money, in measured self-esteem, and in perceived locus of control.

The general picture of group differences that emerges on social variables at age fifteen is that, when compared to the other two groups, more of the Direct Instruction group members reported that they were not socially well-adjusted. More members of the Direct Instruction group reported poor relations with their families and were less likely to seek help for personal problems. Both the lesser degree of sports participation and lack of appointments to an office or job in school suggest that the Direct Instruction group members were less likely than the members of the other two curriculum groups to seek or to receive social acceptance from either peers or teachers through acceptable channels.

Conclusion

Because early childhood education is an important tool to assist the development of young children and improve their life chances as effective and productive members of society, only those programs that are demonstrably effective should be employed. Kagitcibasi, Sunar, and Bekman (1988) found that straightforward custodial care, with routine management, simple physical settings, and large numbers of children per staff member, is simply inappropriate. Findings in the United States from the National Day Care Study (Ruopp, Travers, Glantz, and Coelen, 1979) on staffing ratios lead essentially to the same conclusion. It is possible to say that, when providing services to disadvantaged children, poorly staffed, routine, and poorly supervised programs with poorly trained teachers do not meet the needs of either children or families. Whether the service is in public school programs, Head Start centers, corporate day care, or home day care, we must work to move all programs to a high-quality educational and social development focus.

Implementation of a program focused on high-quality educational and social development for the family and the child is a major challenge. It requires highly trained and supervised staff with small numbers of children per staff member. Extensive commitment to helping the family support the growth of the child, as well as to effective evaluation methods, must be priorities.

This chapter has looked at an important issue in high-quality programs—the curriculum. In the monograph on the High/Scope Preschool Curriculum Comparison study (Weikart, Epstein, Schweinhart, and Bond, 1978), we reached the startling conclusion that insofar as we could measure intellectual and scholastic performance, all three preschool curriculum models appeared to achieve the same positive results in spite of their wide theoretical differences. This outcome was attributed to the fact that all of the programs had similar staffing, training opportunities, supervision, and parent involvement. That is, they met the guidelines for what most observers consider quality programs.

Yet, at age fifteen, when it was possible to begin measuring child outcomes beyond the schools' walls, a striking new finding was discovered. Children who were provided with teacher-directed instruction during the preschool period expressed serious alienation from school, home, and society. At least for disadvantaged youth, just any preschool curriculum will not do. The type of curriculum model employed is critical. Formal academic programs, as represented by teacher-controlled, direct instruction learning models, are inappropriate because, although they have good academic outcomes, they fail to have the desired social-behavioral consequences. Child-initiated learning models, as represented by both the High/Scope curriculum and the traditional nursery school (but not custodial style), offer approaches that lead to both high-quality academic results over the long term and significant improvement in relations with family, school, and society. These programs work because they are developmentally appropriate for the children. Erikson's (1950) theoretical observation that preschool-aged children need to develop a sense of initiative and responsibility is crucial. Physical-social-cognitive development occurs in programs that permit child-initiated learning; it fails to occur when the teacher directs the content and judges the outcome.

Although it would be inappropriate solely on the strength of the High/Scope study to suggest across-the-board curtailment of teacher-directed models in early education programs, the fact that academically oriented direct instruction approaches can be ineffective in reducing children's later social-behavioral problems should be carefully evaluated. It is time to initiate longitudinal studies on the long-term intellectual and social effects of teacher- and child-initiated curriculum approaches in early childhood education. As in the field of medicine, we must conduct rigorous, longitudinal evaluations to uncover the long-term consequences or undesirable side effects of the programs that we create, especially when the programs are different from historically accepted approaches to educating young children.

References

American College Testing Program (ACTP). *User's Guide: Adult Performance Level Survey.* Iowa City: ACTP, 1976.

Bachman, J. G., and Johnston, J. *The Monitoring of the Future Questionnaire.* Ann Arbor: Institute for Social Research, University of Michigan, 1978.

Bereiter, C., and Engelmann, S. *Teaching Disadvantaged Children in the Preschool.* Englewood Cliffs, N.J.: Prentice-Hall, 1966.

Berrueta-Clement, J. R., Schweinhart, L. J., Barnett, W. S., Epstein, A. S., and Weikart, D. P. *Changed Lives: The Effects of the Perry Preschool Program on Youths Through Age 19.* Monographs of the High/Scope Educational Research Foundation, no. 8. Ypsilanti, Mich.: High/Scope Press, 1984.

Consortium for Longitudinal Studies. *As the Twig Is Bent . . . Lasting Effects of Preschool Programs.* Hillsdale, N.J.: Erlbaum, 1983.

DiLorenzo, L. T., Salter, R., and Brady, J. J. *Prekindergarten Programs for Educationally Disadvantaged Children.* Albany: State University of New York Press, 1969.

Empey, L. T. *American Delinquency: Its Meaning and Construction.* Homewood, Ill.: Dorsey, 1978.

Erikson, E. H. *Childhood and Society.* New York: Norton, 1950.

Hohmann, M., Banet, B., and Weikart, D. P. *Young Children in Action: A Manual for Preschool Educators.* Ypsilanti, Mich.: High/Scope Press, 1979.

Kagitcibasi, C., Sunar, D., and Bekman, S. *Comprehensive Preschool Education Project: Final Report.* Ottawa, Ontario, Canada: International Development Research Centre, 1988.

Karnes, M. B., Schwedel, A. M., and Williams, M. B. "A Comparison of Five Approaches for Educating Young Children from Low-Income Homes." In Consortium for Longitudinal Studies, *As the Twig Is Bent . . . Lasting Effects of Preschool Programs.* Hillsdale, N.J.: Erlbaum, 1983.

Kohlberg, L., and Mayer, R. "Development as the Aim of Education." *Harvard Educational Review,* 1972, *42,* 449–496.

McKey, R. H., Condelli, L., Ganson, H., Barrett, B., McConkey, C., and Plantz, M. *The Impact of Head Start on Children, Families and Communities.* Final Report of the Head Start Evaluation, Synthesis, and Utilization Project. Washington, D.C.: CSR, 1985.

Miller, L. B., and Bizzell, R. P. "The Louisville Experiment: A Comparison of Four Programs." In Consortium for Longitudinal Studies, *As the Twig Is Bent . . . Lasting Effects of Preschool Programs.* Hillsdale, N.J.: Erlbaum, 1983.

Morgan, G. *The National State of Child Care Regulation, 1986.* Watertown, Mass.: Work/Family Directions, 1986.

National Association for the Education of Young Children (NAEYC). *Accreditation Criteria and Procedures of the National Academy of Early Childhood Programs.* Washington, D.C.: NAEYC, 1984.

Ruopp, R., Travers, J., Glantz, F., and Coelen, C. *Children at the Center: Summary Findings and Their Implications.* Final Report of the National Day Care Study, Vol. 1. Cambridge, Mass.: ABT Associates, 1979.

Schweinhart, L. J., Weikart, D. P., and Larner, M. B. "Consequences of Three Preschool Curriculum Models Through Age 15." *Early Childhood Research Quarterly,* 1986, *1,* 15–45.

Terman, L. M., and Merrill, M. A. *Stanford-Binet Intelligence Scale, Form L-M: Manual for the Third Revision.* Boston: Houghton Mifflin, 1970.

Tiegs, E. W., and Clark, W. W. *California Achievement Tests: 1957 Edition with 1963 Norms.* Monterey, Calif.: California Test Bureau, 1963.

Waldman, S. "The Stingy Politics of Head Start." *Newsweek,* Fall/Winter 1990, pp. 78–79.

Wechsler, D. *Wechsler Intelligence Scale for Children.* New York: Psychological Corporation, 1949.

Weikart, D. P. "Relationship of Curriculum, Teaching, and Learning in Preschool Education." In J. C. Stanley (ed.), *Preschool Programs for the Disadvantaged.* Baltimore, Md.: Johns Hopkins University Press, 1972.

Weikart, D. P., Epstein, A. S., Schweinhart, L. J., and Bond, J. *The Ypsilanti Preschool Curriculum Demonstration Project: Preschool Years and Longitudinal Results.* Monographs of the High/Scope Educational Research Foundation, no. 4. Ypsilanti, Mich.: High/Scope Press, 1978.

Whitebook, M., Howes, C., and Phillips, D. *Who Cares? Child Care Teachers and the Quality of Care in America.* Final Report of the National Child Care Staffing Study. Oakland, Calif.: Child Care Employee Project, 1989.

David P. Weikart is president of High/Scope Educational Research Foundation in Ypsilanti, Michigan, a nonprofit research, development, and training organization. In 1962 he initiated the Perry Preschool Project to study the long-term results of high-quality early childhood education on the growth and development of young children through adulthood.

Lawrence J. Schweinhart is chair of High/Scope's research division and has worked at High/Scope since 1975. With David P. Weikart, he directs the High/Scope Perry Preschool Project and Preschool Curriculum Comparison study.

How developmentally appropriate are public school classrooms for four-year-old disadvantaged children?

Public School Preschools and the Disadvantaged

Dale C. Farran, Beverly Silveri, Anne Culp

Recently, there has been an increase in the level of public support for governmental provision of educational intervention programs, particularly for economically disadvantaged children, giving rise to concerns over what sort of focus these programs should have. The debate also centers on *where* to house intervention programs (Committee for Economic Development, 1987; Kagan, 1988; Schorr, 1988; Schweinhart, Koshel, and Bridgeman, 1987), and many have suggested that the public schools are the appropriate sites (for example, Futrell, 1987; Hymes, 1987; Mitchell and Modigliani, 1989).

While the debate continues in the press and on the floors of state legislatures, local school systems are in the process of establishing preschool programs for disadvantaged children in an ever-growing number of states. In a nationwide survey of this trend, Marx and Seligson (1988) found a threefold increase in the number of states (from ten states to twenty-seven) with state-funded prekindergarten programs between 1984 and 1987. Federal money is also being redirected from school-age programs to preschools at the discretion of local school systems.

One danger to this "overnight" grassroots implementation of preschool programs in the public schools is that there are no current data that speak to their quality or effectiveness. Opponents of public school prekindergarten programs believe that acceptance of such programs is characterized more by "enthusiasm than thought" (Zigler, 1987, p. 254). Parents may support public school involvement because quality child care is scarce and expensive, or because they may perceive all child care to be inherently unreliable; therefore, the reliability of the public schools becomes a very attractive component of a preschool program. Furthermore, parents are oriented to

NEW DIRECTIONS FOR CHILD DEVELOPMENT, no. 53, Fall 1991 © Jossey-Bass Inc., Publishers

public schools for educating their older children and may feel that they are feasible and convenient places for their younger children as well.

There is disagreement among professionals about how academic the focus of these programs should be. Preschool programs like Head Start are housed at the state level in departments of health and human services; public education has traditionally dealt with older children. Therefore, early education housed in the public schools will be under the auspices of educators who may not be knowledgeable about the developmental needs of young children and who may perceive such programs as a downward extension of elementary education (Elkind, 1983; Zimiles, 1986). Thus, Morgan (1985) warns that prekindergarten programs in public schools will involve a narrow focus on direct instruction in academic skills instead of a broad focus on developmentally appropriate activities.

These concerns are felt even more sharply by advocates for African-American children, many of whom believe that the public schools have failed to meet the needs of nonwhite ethnic children (Moore, 1987). For example, a recent study in North Carolina found that although African-American children entered first grade comparatively equal to their white counterparts, by the end of the first grade they were doing less well, with the gap widening as the children progressed through school (Parker, 1988). Researchers such as Ogbu (1986) have argued that consciously and unconsciously textbooks and curricula teach black and white children their respective places in American society. Advocates for African-American children question whether parents should subject their young children to beginning on the lower rung of this educational system any earlier than is necessary (Moore, 1987).

While data on the effectiveness of these programs for ensuring a solid education and later employability may be persuasive to policymakers and school administrators, those achievements in education and employment have, in fact, been accomplished by only a few high-quality programs conducted some time ago, none of which was housed in the public schools. It is likely that the majority of the children who will be enrolled in public school preschool programs will be from minority groups, and most of those children will be African-American. The need for developmentally appropriate practices is even more urgent for this population (Anderson, 1988), but the needs of minority children and children from different subcultural groups typically have not been addressed in position statements on developmentally appropriate practices (for example, National Association for the Education of Young Children, 1986; Southern Association on Children Under Six, 1986). Even if teachers wanted to avoid placing the wrong kinds of academic stress on the children, it is not clear what a developmentally appropriate preschool, housed in the public schools and intended for educationally disadvantaged children, should look like.

This chapter focuses on a two-year study of the implementation of public school preschools for disadvantaged children in one region of North Carolina. We examine both the effects of the programs on the children's skills and the kinds of classroom environments provided. Our goal is to provide preliminary descriptive information that addresses the question of whether these classrooms are developmentally appropriate for the children that are served.

The Preschool Initiative Network

In 1988, the Z. Smith Reynolds Foundation in North Carolina funded a project aimed at creating a support network among public school preschool teachers in one region of the state (Farran, 1988). In the first year, eleven classrooms in five school districts were involved. Funding for the second year allowed the program to expand to thirty-one classrooms in eight school districts; these were all the prekindergarten programs sponsored by the state's Department of Public Instruction in the region. The goal of the network was to collect information in collaboration with the teachers that would help them make their classrooms developmentally appropriate for disadvantaged four-year-olds.

Demographic Data. During the first year, demographic data were compiled by the teachers for the children in their classrooms. Results showed that all the children were from disadvantaged homes; family income averaged $10,470 (income figures were available for 72 percent of the sample). Most of the mothers of these children worked (61 percent) and had at least a high school diploma (77 percent). In these preschools, 74 percent of the children were black, 23 percent were white, and 3 percent were "other." Gender distribution was nearly equal, with 46 percent of the children being female. By teacher estimation, 49 percent of the children lived with both their fathers and mothers, 44 percent lived with their single mothers (either alone or with significant others), and 7 percent lived with neither of their parents (this information on home environment was available for 75 percent of the sample).

The picture that these statistics present is different from the picture of the populations of earlier intervention programs insofar as the parents of the children in the North Carolina programs had attained higher levels of education and had jobs. Unfortunately, their economic status does not seem to be different from that of participants in earlier programs of the 1960s and 1970s, as the families continue to be impoverished.

Assessments of the Children. In the first year of the study, children were individually assessed at the beginning and end of the school year with the Peabody Picture Vocabulary Test (PPVT), which is an assessment of receptive vocabulary, and the McCarthy Scales of Children's Abilities (with the four subscales verbal, perceptual, quantitative, and memory).

Overall, there were significant changes over time in the test scores of these disadvantaged children in preschool classrooms in the public schools, both on the PPVT and on the verbal and perceptual subscales of the McCarthy. The improvement on receptive vocabulary as measured by the PPVT (from ninth percentile in the fall to eighteenth percentile in the spring) was more substantial than the improvement on any subscale of the McCarthy. Children's quantitative and memory performances did not show increases over time.

In addition to a general effect of time in the classroom, we obtained a significant effect for classroom, indicating that not all the classrooms were achieving the same results. Teachers did not all achieve the same results on receptive language skills as assessed by PPVT standard scores. Gains across classrooms on the PPVT ranged from 1.6 points to 17.1 points, making it clear that some of the classrooms were much more effective than were others at helping children master receptive vocabulary. The variability across the classrooms and the lack of increase in quantitative and memory skills made it imperative to examine the interactions between adults and children within these preschools.

Classroom Organization. In the second year, extensive classroom observation data were collected using a scale developed for this project. The scale combines Parten's (1932) play categories with a system for observing in open classrooms (Farran, 1977). The *Manual for Observation of Play in Preschools (MOPP)* (Culp and Farran, 1989) is intended to be used during center-based or free-play time, the period during the day when teachers have the children freely circulate and use materials available in the class at various play centers. *MOPP* uses an event-sampling technique; judgments about physical location, proximity to others, level of play, affect, and incidence of talking are made about each child in turn. A "sweep" consists of taking data on all children in the class; ten sweeps can be accomplished in forty-five to sixty minutes.

Classrooms were observed in February 1990 and again in May 1990. We present results here based on four categories from *MOPP*: physical location, interactive nature of play, teacher presence, and amount of talking.

In terms of physical location, when children were actually in play centers during "center time," the two sites most frequently observed were art and blocks (each comprising about 10 percent of the observations at both times). However, children spent relatively little time using the centers: In these classrooms the most commonly observed physical location for the children during free-play time was sitting in a large group. In the February observation, children were observed in a large group 20 percent of the free-play time. Teachers were given this information in March and urged to restrict the use of large groups; in May, the percentage of time devoted to large groups was only slightly reduced, with 15 percent of free-play time spent in large groups. (It is important to note that this is the percentage of *center-based* activity devoted to large groups, not the occurrence of large-group activity; one can assume that large-group activities occurred much more often than 15 percent of the total day.)

In terms of the interactive nature of play in February, when children were not in large groups they engaged in parallel play (using Parten's definition) 25 percent of the time: They were near another child, engaged with material but not playing with the other child(ren). For 23 percent of the observations, children were participating in associative play, engaged both with other children and with materials. Cooperative play (following rules) was observed less than 1 percent of the time. By May, the amount of parallel play had increased (to 37 percent of observations), associative play had decreased (to 19 percent), and cooperative play had disappeared. If one assumes that associative and cooperative play are the more developmentally advanced play states, there was considerable regression in these classrooms.

In terms of teacher presence and child verbalization, during center time (exclusive of the time in large groups) children were in proximity to the teachers 29 percent of the time, although the range across the classrooms was 16-57 percent. Proximity here means being near a teacher; it does not mean *interacting* with the teacher. In 20 percent of the observations, children were observed verbalizing, with a range across classrooms of 10-34 percent. Classrooms therefore varied widely in terms of the accessibility of the teacher and the degree of verbal participation of the children. It is our contention that given the developmental needs of these children, facilitation of sustained verbal interactions with adults should be one of the primary goals for these classrooms.

The interactions among these behavioral states are currently being analyzed. For example, when the teacher was near, children addressed 50 percent of their verbalizations to him or her, indicating that the teacher was a potent elicitor of talk from the children. Cooperative play occurred *only* in the presence of a teacher in these classrooms, and when the teacher was nearby, the amount of associative play increased. Associative play can be seen as a developmentally important activity; approximately 66 percent of the observed talking occurred when the children were engaged in associative play. It is also important to note that the type of talk that occurred in the play centers was qualitatively different from the type of talk that was observed in large groups. In large groups, singing and simple declaratives made up the bulk of verbalizations; questions (the most complex verbal category coded) occurred *only* in the centers.

The picture of these classrooms that emerges from the observational data is one where children spent time with the teacher in large-group activity but spent little time *interacting* with adults or children during free play. The teacher appeared to act as an important facilitator of developmentally advanced behavior. Associative play occurred more when a teacher was present. Associative play is important because the most talking and the most developmentally advanced levels of talking in these classrooms occurred during associative play at centers. Over time, however, the children engaged in considerably less associative play.

Parallel activities may be good preparation for the expectations of an academically focused kindergarten and first grade, where children do worksheets and are quiet. The problem is that parallel play does not offer children the opportunity to engage in the kinds of complex interactions (particularly verbal ones) that we believe are likely to advance the underlying skills needed for future learning. These underlying skills include such cognitive skills as causal reasoning through hypothesis-testing dialogues and joint problem solving, and such social skills as turn taking, sharing, and learning others' perspectives. The lack of these experiences in the classroom may be more damaging for disadvantaged children, who may not be receiving compensatory interactions outside of class.

"Developmentally Appropriate" Is Not a Singular Concept

The experiences provided by these new public school classrooms may be critical for the future success of the disadvantaged children that they serve. Our data describe classrooms that may be functioning in ways that the teachers believe are "developmentally appropriate," given the lack of clarity in the definition of that term. In fact, a recent survey of public school preschool teachers (Silveri, 1989) indicated that the teachers believed that developmental appropriateness meant allowing the children to engage freely with materials *without teacher involvement,* that teachers should not be asking questions of the children, and that an understanding of numerical concepts was not as important as language development. Teachers were indecisive about whether the children's backgrounds should affect the activities offered in the classrooms. Results from the classrooms we observed were consistent with these points of view. Teachers did not appear to be able to distinguish their own noninvolvement from overly and inappropriately academic involvement, and they also did not appear to know how to engage responsively with children in ways that facilitate their learning about a variety of topics (including numeracy). Consequently, their role in these classrooms could best be described as "monitor."

This uncertainty about the "developmental appropriateness" of activities may be less a teachers' problem than a problem for the early childhood profession in its failure to provide an adequate and complete discussion of the term. It is important to realize that there cannot be a single definition of developmental appropriateness, not if children's individual needs are truly to be taken into account. (It is perhaps easier to define *in*appropriate activities: pedagogically driven—that is, academic—activities are inappropriate for children under age seven.) Appropriate activities depend not just on the ages of the children but also on their experiential backgrounds, learning styles, temperaments, and so forth. The search for a single, all-inclusive definition may be fruitless; what teachers need to know is how to recognize when children are learning and responding to the social and physical environments provided and how to change those environments if they fail to stimulate the children.

Conclusion

The rapidity with which preschool programs have been implemented in local public school systems over the past three to five years is astounding. It suggests that local school administrators have perceived both a need and a solution almost simultaneously. But we must ask whether the "solution" actually is valid. Without attention to the developmental nature of the programs offered, we do not believe that they will work.

The classrooms must be developmentally appropriate to the age range of the children for whom they are intended, an age range with which the public schools have not dealt before. Preschool children need fundamentally different educational experiences than those provided to older children. Moreover, the programs must also be developmentally appropriate for the needs of the individual children served. Because these programs are intended for disadvantaged minority children, it is crucial that the special backgrounds of those children be taken into account in designing the classroom and the curriculum.

Both of these factors mandate a high level of teacher training and support. Because the North Carolina programs, like those in many other areas, have been started on the local school district level, we are concerned that insufficient support has been given to them at a more general statewide or regional level. If more support is not provided, this may be a very short-lived experiment, with the wrong kind of information learned from it. Time is of the essence in determining how to help teachers create the kinds of environments that will benefit children in need of a positive beginning to their educational careers.

References

Anderson, J. A. "Cognitive Styles and Multicultural Populations." *Journal of Teacher Education*, 1988, *39*, 2–9.

Committee for Economic Development (CED). *Children in Need: Investment Strategies for the Educationally Disadvantaged*. New York: CED, 1987.

Culp, A., and Farran, D. C. *Manual for Observation of Play in Preschools*. Greensboro: Department of Child Development and Family Relations, University of North Carolina, 1989.

Elkind, N. J. "The Long-Term Effectiveness of Early Intervention." In E. M. Goetz and K. E. Allen (eds.), *Early Childhood Education: Special Environmental, Policy, and Legal Considerations*. Baltimore, Md.: Aspen, 1983.

Farran, D. C. "Young Children's Behavior in Open Classrooms." *Forum on Open Education*, 1977, *13*, 1–12.

Farran, D. C. "The Preschool Initiative Network." Unpublished grant proposal funded by the Z. Smith Reynolds Foundation, Winston-Salem, North Carolina, 1988.

Futrell, M. H. "Public Schools and Four-Year-Olds: A Teacher's View." *American Psychologist*, 1987, *42* (3), 251–253.

Hymes, J. L. "Public Schools for Four-Year-Olds." *Young Children*, 1987, *42*, 51–52.

Kagan, S. L. "Current Reforms in Early Childhood Education: Are We Addressing the Issues?" *Young Children*, 1988, *43*, 27–32.

Marx, F., and Seligson, M. *The Public School Early Childhood Study: The State Survey.* New York: Bank Street College, 1988.

Mitchell, A., and Modigliani, K. "Young Children in Public Schools?" *Young Children*, 1989, *44*, 56–61.

Moore, E. "Childcare in the Public Schools: Public Accountability and the Black Child." In S. L. Kagan and E. F. Zigler (eds.), *Early Schooling: The National Debate.* New Haven, Conn.: Yale University Press, 1987.

Morgan, G. "Programs for Young Children in Public Schools? Only If . . . " *Young Children*, 1985, *40*, 54.

National Association for the Education of Young Children (NAEYC). *Position Statement on Developmentally Appropriate Practice in Early Childhood Programs Serving Children from Birth Through Age 8.* Washington, D.C.: NAEYC, 1986.

Ogbu, J. U. "Castelike Stratification as a Risk Factor for Mental Retardation in the United States." In D. C. Farran and J. D. McKinney (eds.), *Risk in Intellectual and Psychosocial Development.* San Diego, Calif.: Academic Press, 1986.

Parker, D. A. "Underachievement in North Carolina." A report prepared for the Greensboro affiliate of the National Black Child Development Institute, Greensboro, North Carolina, 1988.

Parten, M. B. "Social Participation Among Preschool Children." *Journal of Abnormal and Social Psychology*, 1932, *27*, 243–269.

Schorr, L. *Within Our Reach: Breaking the Cycle of Disadvantage.* New York: Anchor, 1988.

Schweinhart, L. J., Koshel, J. J., and Bridgeman, A. "Policy Options for Preschool Programs." *Phi Delta Kappan*, 1987, *68*, 524–529.

Silveri, B. "What Do You Think?" Survey administered at Share Day for the Preschool Initiative Network, Department of Child Development and Family Relations, University of North Carolina, Greensboro, December 1989.

Southern Association for Children Under Six. "Position Statement on Quality Four-Year-Old Programs in Public Schools." *Dimensions*, 1986, *14*, 28.

Zigler, E. F. "Formal Schooling for Four-Year-Olds? No." *American Psychologist*, 1987, *42* (3), 254–260.

Zimiles, H. "Rethinking the Role of Research: New Issues and Lingering Doubts in an Era of Expanding Preschool Education." *Early Childhood Research Quarterly*, 1986, *1*, 189–206.

Dale C. Farran is professor of child development and chair of the Department of Child Development and Family Relations at the University of North Carolina, Greensboro. Her research interests involve the development of language and school readiness skills in children from at-risk conditions and the effects of intervention.

Beverly Silveri is completing her master's degree in child development and family relations at the University of North Carolina, Greensboro. Her focus is on the development of African-American children and the appropriateness of preschool programs.

Anne Culp is a human development specialist in the College of Home Economics, Oklahoma State University, Stillwater. Her research focuses on at-risk children and language development.

*Public schools must move beyond narrow academic goals to become
a comprehensive child care and family support system.*

Beyond Academic Instruction:
The Twenty-First-Century School Model
for Preschoolers

Edward F. Zigler, Elizabeth Gilman

Contrary to the outcry of many social commentators, the American family
is not going to die. It is going to do better or it is going to do worse; its
future course depends on whether we can institutionalize the infrastructure
necessary to make the new American family functional. The adaptation of
our society to the new family has not kept pace with the rapid changes
experienced by that family. As a result, the need for high-quality child care
and family support has reached crisis proportions.

Two striking demographic changes have occurred in the past decade:
One is the increasing percentage of women in the out-of-home work force;
the other is the rise in the number of single-parent homes. Today, 65
percent of American mothers of school-aged children are in the out-of-
home work force. Among mothers of preschoolers, that number is 57 percent (Children's Defense Fund, 1990a). More striking still is the fact that
52 percent of mothers of babies under one year of age are working outside
the home. Nor is this trend likely to abate: A recent projection indicates
that by 1995, between 75 and 80 percent of all school-aged children will
have mothers in the out-of-home work force (Hofferth and Phillips, 1987).
The fact is that we have come to a time in the United States when most
two-parent homes require two incomes for survival.

The second major change in the American family is in the number of
single-parent homes. The term "single-parent home" is really a euphemism:
Over 90 percent of these homes are headed by women. Of the marriages
that take place this year, our best prediction is that 50 percent of them will

NEW DIRECTIONS FOR CHILD DEVELOPMENT, no. 53, Fall 1991 © Jossey-Bass Inc., Publishers

end in divorce. Today in the United States, one of every four children is being raised in a single-parent home. Among our black citizens, that number is well over 50 percent. Families headed by women made up 53 percent of our poor families in 1988 (Children's Defense Fund, 1990b). These single parents, most of them mothers, must work or rely on welfare. Child care is their greatest need.

We now have in this country the Family Support Act, which is intended to remove mothers from the Aid to Families with Dependent Children program and incorporate them into the work force. In order for such a program to work, we must provide adequate care for the children of these mothers. It would be a disaster if we were to take mothers from the home in order to place them into training or work, while placing their children in settings of such low quality that we would virtually guarantee another generation on welfare. The success of the Family Support Act, and indeed of the family itself in America, depends on our having in place an effective, high-quality, child care system.

Quality of Child Care in America

What is the state of the child care our children are now receiving? In terms of quality, it is very heterogeneous. Probably the most comprehensive study done in the last ten years on the quality of child care, the National Child Care Staffing study (Whitebook, Howes, and Phillips, 1989) assessed child care centers all over America and found that the average quality was poor. Every day in this country, hundreds of thousands of children are placed in settings that compromise their optimal growth and development. Individuals caring for our children are not adequately trained or adequately paid and certainly have no social status: 70 percent of workers in the child care system in America work below the minimum wage. The annual employee turnover rate in the American child care system is about the same as that of filling station attendants, about 40 percent. Children need continuity of care and clearly they cannot receive it with this high turnover rate.

The National Child Care Staffing study revealed a three-tiered system of child care. As expected, the affluent purchase the best care for their children. Surprisingly, poor children receive the next best level of care, because of Title XX, subsidies, charitable contributions, and the like. The worst child care in America is received by the children of the mainstream, the lower-middle class and the working class. Although some people hoped that day-care regulation would guarantee quality, a Children's Defense Fund (1990a) analysis reveals that state regulations across the country are so inadequate that they actually guarantee the neglect of children. Thus, the evidence reveals that the vast majority of young children are growing up in low-quality child care environments.

Twenty-First-Century School Model—More Than Academics

Our proposed solution to this problem is simple. The Twenty-First-Century School model would build child care and family support into the existing school system (Zigler, 1989). Education in America once resembled the state of child care today: Few children were fortunate enough to receive an adequate education. The nation decided that this was unacceptable and provided for a minimum level of education for all citizens. Today, day care is a disorganized, incoherent collection of hundreds of thousands of settings and services. Such a hodge-podge approach will never work, and no amount of tinkering with the present nonsystem will make it work. Thirty years of failure in this country to establish a coherent child care system is enough, especially when the victims of this failure are our children.

School Buildings as Resources. One means of simplifying and organizing this system is to use as its core a known and trusted institution, the school. We have in this country a $1–2 trillion investment in school buildings. In the past, these buildings have been used to implement only a narrow set of academic goals. There is every reason to utilize these buildings more fully, both for early childhood services and for after-school programs. This is the idea behind the Twenty-First-Century School model. The school need not bear the burden of providing extra services; each community has the option of using existing school personnel or contracting for services. Existing programs, such as Head Start or other preschool or after-school services, can be incorporated into the system; local communities can contract for other services as needed. Every component of the Twenty-First-Century School model already exists; all the parts of the concept have been researched and their value demonstrated. To resolve our preschool and school-aged child care problems, we have only to combine these components in a comprehensive, organized manner.

First, we must stop thinking of the school as it has been used in the past, open for formal schooling during limited hours, used only nine months a year. Rather, the school must be seen as a free-standing building that exists in every neighborhood. In each of these buildings, we can establish a family support and child care system, along with the formal schooling that already takes place there. The first system, that of the formal school, would be open from eight o'clock in the morning until school closing at three o'clock in the afternoon, nine months a year. The second system—the family support and child care system—would be open from seven o'clock in the morning until six o'clock in the evening, twelve months a year. The family support system would begin at the birth of a child and would extend to age twelve. All-day preschool child care could be available for all families who need it. Those who do not need a full day could elect child care as required. Mothers who do not work outside the home could use this as a nursery school. Within the Twenty-First-Century School system, school-aged children of working parents would receive appropriate supervision and planned activities after their school day.

Outreach Programs. Three outreach programs are integral to the Twenty-First-Century School model, with parental involvement a key factor in all of them. The first is a birth-to-age-three program that includes home visitation, parental education, and health and developmental assistance. This birth-to-three model is already in place as the Parents As Teachers (PAT) program in Missouri. The project's success has been demonstrated: PAT children do better in early life and these children are performing better in school (Missouri Department of Elementary and Secondary Education, 1985).

The second outreach program consists of family day-care homes. These homes, in which a parent takes in several children in addition to his or her own, are very common throughout America. Their quality, however, is extremely uneven. Here we find the best and the worst care in the nation, with great variation in the applicable state regulations. One problem is the isolation of each of the family homes and the difficulty of monitoring the quality of day care received. Within the Twenty-First-Century School model, day-care homes would be tied into a community network, which would use the school facility as the hub of the network responsible for the training, monitoring, and support of the family day-care parents.

As a third outreach program, each school would contain an information-and-referral system for parents. It would be quite inexpensive for personnel in the Twenty-First-Century School to assist parents in finding such services as night care for children, inoculations for measles, eye examinations, food stamps, or family counseling—free or inexpensive services that often exist in a community but that many parents, particularly poor parents, do not realize are available.

Twenty-First-Century School Model for Preschoolers

As we think about bringing prekindergarten children into the Twenty-First-Century School, it is essential that we keep the idea of "developmentally appropriate practices" for young children (Bredekamp, 1987) in the forefront of our thinking. Many social commentators have noted that children today are growing up too fast. Placing four- and five-year-olds into full-day public school-based education programs may only compound this problem, if we are not careful. The pressing need for child care to serve preschoolers should not lead us to place children in programs that are inappropriate or harmful. As Elkind (1987) has argued, formal and highly structured academic programs for young children deny them the opportunity to develop at their own pace, to learn through self-directed exploration, and to develop confidence in themselves as learners.

Early childhood programs in the twenty-first century will need to provide both high-quality child care and high-quality education. The models of the past—the custodial care provided in day-care centers for children of working parents, early intervention programs for disadvantaged children, and private nursery schools for middle-class children—need to be replaced by a more comprehensive model serving a wide spectrum of children. We need to replace custodial care for children of working parents with developmentally enriching early childhood education. The polarization of mainstream and underclass in our society makes it increasingly important that we move away from our racially and socioeconomically segregated early childhood system toward a more integrated model.

In essence, there is no real distinction between high-quality child care and what we refer to as good preschool intervention. Everyone seems to love Head Start and other intervention programs today, yet the desirability of child care is still questioned by some. Caldwell (1974) has suggested that we stop using the term "child care" with its babysitting connotations and adopt the term "educare." This is an appealing idea because that is what occurs in the preschool period. Preschool education provides the foundation on which subsequent learning takes place. A high-quality program for three-, four-, and five-year-olds is by definition an educational program, a program that meets the cognitive, social, emotional, and physical needs of the young child by being developmentally appropriate and not overly structured.

Cost-Benefit Analysis

Although we know what makes for a successful early childhood program, cost is unfortunately the stumbling block in our efforts to improve child care and education for young children (Zigler and Lang, 1991). Yet, we must become aware of what benefits we can purchase with these costs. These benefits are detailed in the Cornell consortium's analysis of several major intervention efforts (Darlington, Royce, Snipper, Murray, and Lazar, 1980; Consortium for Longitudinal Studies, 1983), and in a follow-up study of one of these efforts, High/Scope (Berrueta-Clement, Schweinhart, Barnett, Epstein, and Weikart, 1984). Among the numerous benefits found from early intervention were children at their correct grade level for age, fewer children in special education programs, fewer program graduates on welfare, more graduates going on to college, and a decrease in delinquency and criminality (Zigler, Taussig, and Black, 1990). It has been shown that for every dollar invested in preschool education, a subsequent four-dollar saving can be identified (Berrueta-Clement, Schweinhart, Barnett, Epstein, and Weikart, 1984; Barnett, 1985). That is the proper way to approach the Twenty-First-Century School, not so much as a cost to be assessed but as an investment in what economists refer to as human capital. Human resources in large part are our children; if society wants to have productive workers in its future, we must invest in our children today.

The costs of the Twenty-First-Century School can be met in a variety of ways. For the middle class, fees can be assessed on a sliding scale. For the children of the poor, who need this model the most, some federal funding sources could be made available (for example, Title XX, Chapter I, and Head Start). States are also becoming aware that if we expect to have a generation of productive citizens, we must invest in preschool and later child care in exactly the same way as we have invested in formal schooling. Communities in several states (Missouri, Connecticut, Colorado, Kansas, and Wyoming) have already established models of the full Twenty-First-Century School program. Other communities, such as Los Angeles, have adopted before- and after-school care for all of their children. Finally, the business sector has begun to feel the need for a coherent child care system, recognizing that the greatest barrier to entrance into the work force of women not already working outside the home is the absence of high-quality, affordable child care.

Conclusion

Despite these sound economic justifications for the Twenty-First-Century School model, the primary social policy reason for instituting decent pre-school and child care programs for our children must be the humane nature of the cause. The ultimate assessment of the success of the Twenty-First-Century School, or of any intervention model, is not whether the child's IQ has changed by five points. It is whether the child displays everyday social competence by meeting social expectancies, advancing appropriately in school, and staying out of trouble. Success should be measured by whether the child has a good self-image and a high level of aspiration (Zigler and Trickett, 1978). With these social tools, the child has an opportunity to grow into his or her potential and to lead a fulfilling life. What we have learned in over thirty years of early intervention programs is that there is no quick way to optimize the growth and development of a child. Nor is there a magic, one-year period in which intervention must take place (Zigler and Berman, 1983). Supportive parenting, comprehensive health care, developmentally appropriate schooling, and good child care must persist throughout childhood. Each of the services within the Twenty-First-Century model may be initiated individually and later built upon, as community need and budgetary constraints dictate. The strengths of the program, and its ultimate effectiveness, lie in its comprehensive nature, its use of existing resources, and its close involvement with parents and the community that it serves. Such a program constitutes a humane and cost-effective response to the needs of America's children and families.

References

Barnett, W. S. *The Perry Preschool Project and Its Long-Term Effects: A Benefit-Cost Analysis*. High/Scope Early Childhood Policy Papers, no. 2. Ypsilanti, Mich.: High/Scope Press, 1985.

Berrueta-Clement, J. R., Schweinhart, L. J., Barnett, W. S., Epstein, A. S., and Weikart, D. P. *Changed Lives: The Effects of the Perry Preschool Program on Youths Through Age 19*. Monographs of the High/Scope Educational Research Foundation, no. 8. Ypsilanti, Mich.: High/Scope Press, 1984.

Bredekamp, S. E. (ed.). *Developmentally Appropriate Practice in Early Childhood Programs Serving Children from Birth Through Age 8*. Washington, D.C.: National Association for the Education of Young Children, 1987.

Caldwell, B. M. "A Decade of Early Intervention Programs: What We Have Learned." *American Journal of Orthopsychiatry*, 1974, *44*, 491-496.

Children's Defense Fund. *Children 1990: A Report Card, Briefing Book, and Action Primer*. Washington, D.C.: Children's Defense Fund, 1990a.

Children's Defense Fund. *S.O.S. America! A Children's Defense Budget*. Washington, D.C.: National Association for the Education of Young Children, 1990b.

Consortium for Longitudinal Studies. *As the Twig Is Bent . . . Lasting Effects of Preschool Programs*. Hillsdale, N.J.: Erlbaum, 1983.

Darlington, R. B., Royce, J. M., Snipper, A. S., Murray, H., and Lazar, I. "Preschool Programs and Later School Competence of Children from Low-Income Families." *Science*, 1980, *208*, 202-204.

Elkind, D. "Early Childhood Education on Its Own Terms." In S. L. Kagan and E. F. Zigler (eds.), *Early Schooling: The National Debate*. New Haven, Conn.: Yale University Press, 1987.

Hofferth, S., and Phillips, D. A. "Child Care in the United States, 1970 to 1995." *Journal of Marriage and the Family*, 1987, *49*, 559-571.

Missouri Department of Elementary and Secondary Education. *Evaluation Report: New Parents as Teachers Project*. Jefferson City: Missouri Department of Elementary and Secondary Education, 1985.

Whitebook, M., Howes, C., and Phillips, D. *Who Cares? Child Care Teachers and the Quality of Care in America*. Final Report of the National Child Care Staffing Study. Oakland, Calif.: Child Care Employee Project, 1989.

Zigler, E. F. "Addressing the Nation's Child Care Crisis: The School of the Twenty-First Century." *American Journal of Orthopsychiatry*, 1989, *59*, 484-491.

Zigler, E. F., and Berman, W. "Discerning the Future of Early Childhood Intervention." *American Psychologist*, 1983, *38*, 894-906.

Zigler, E. F., and Lang, M. E. *Child Care Choices: Balancing the Needs of Children, Families, and Society*. New York: Free Press, 1991.

Zigler, E. F., Taussig, C. L., and Black, K. B. "Early Childhood Intervention: A Promising Preventative for Juvenile Delinquency." Unpublished manuscript, Bush Center in Child Development and Social Policy, Yale University, 1990.

Zigler, E. F., and Trickett, P. K. "IQ, Social Competence, and Evaluation of Early Childhood Intervention Programs." *American Psychologist*, 1978, *33*, 789-798.

Edward F. Zigler is Sterling Professor of Psychology at Yale University, where he also serves as director of the Bush Center in Child Development and Social Policy.

Elizabeth Gilman is postdoctoral associate in psychology at Yale University and a fellow of the Bush Center in Child Development and Social Policy.

Debates over early academic programs reflect diverse beliefs about
how to influence the trajectory of development.

Preschool Education:
For Whom and Why?

Irving E. Sigel

The chapters in this volume reflect different social, political, and educational aspects of preschool programs. Rescorla, Hyson, and Hirsh-Pasek (Chapters One to Five) present the issue of the "academic preschool," most relevant to a middle-class group of parents interested in fostering academic success for their children as a long-term objective. In contrast, Weikart and Schweinhart (Chapter Seven) report the outcomes of preschool education for children of the underclass. Stipek (Chapter Six) presents a typology of preschool programs as a basis for examining the occurrence and characteristics of didactic or "academic" early childhood classrooms. Her findings are useful in conceptualizing preschool education in relation to educational objectives. Farran, Silveri, and Culp (Chapter Eight) critically examine the developmental appropriateness of preschool education for disadvantaged children within public school settings. Finally, Zigler and Gilman (Chapter Nine) place the issue of preschool education in the context of child care broadly conceived as a social program. Their report is a visionary, futuristic approach that encompasses the entire field of child care.

The chapters highlight three major questions in preschool education. First, what is the function of preschool education? That is, what are the beliefs and values underlying the idea of institutionalized education experiences for young children? Second, what target populations does early childhood education serve, and, given these different target groups, what kinds of programs might be most appropriate? Third, does preschool make a difference, and, more specifically, what kinds of practices make a difference for what areas of development and for what kinds of target populations?

NEW DIRECTIONS FOR CHILD DEVELOPMENT, no. 53, Fall 1991 © Jossey-Bass Inc., Publishers

Why Preschool Education? The Trajectory Principle

Underlying all of the authors' efforts is the implicitly accepted proposition that preschool experience is not only good but also desirable. This proposition is based on what I refer to as the *trajectory principle,* which states that early experiences influence the trajectory of later development. What is done to children during these formative years leaves some impression on the quality and quantity of their growth in social, emotional, and cognitive domains.

The trajectory principle permeates our culture in general, and education in particular. This dynamic orientation places little emphasis on the ongoing present, so that preschool is a place to engage in and enjoy not for the sake of the "now" but rather for the sake of its future influence on children. The institution of the preschool is justified because of what it can contribute to the child's development toward adulthood. The chapters in this volume by Rescorla, Hyson, and Hirsh-Pasek present data that are consistent with this future-oriented justification for preschool education. Their research clearly illustrates that, for most parents, young children's education is a preparation for the social or educational future.

Influencing the Trajectory. Once the trajectory principle is accepted, the next step is to determine the kinds of educational programs that can achieve the short- and long-term goals (whatever they may be) of the preschool experience. The program choices that are made for influencing the trajectory are based on the program developer's conceptual orientation. For some, the guidelines are loose and unspecified, whereas for others, like Weikart and Schweinhart, Piaget was a seminal figure. For Bereiter and Engelmann (1966) or for the Darcee program, a social behavioral framework served as the conceptual guide (Miller and Dyer, 1975). The Bank Street model (Shapiro and Biber, 1972) was influenced by Freud and Werner. Program diversity evolves in part because of the different conceptual frameworks of program developers.

The academic preschool is probably based on the proposition that if a child starts early, he or she will get ahead of the game and enter kindergarten with many advantages in knowledge and in problem-solving skills. This point of view reflects the notion that accumulation of knowledge and skills provides the enabling tools for academic success. The most vocal and extreme advocates of this view are Glenn Doman and his colleagues (Doman, Doman, and Aisen, 1985). They write, "Those first six years of life are *the* critical years because, by six, we have laid the groundwork for what we are to be" (Doman, Doman, and Aisen, 1985, p. 37). They have laid out a curriculum in which parents begin at infancy to teach children to read, to do math, and to develop a vocabulary, claiming that "babies can learn absolutely anything that you can present to them in an honest and factual way and they don't give a fig whether it is encyclopedic knowledge, reading words, math, or nonsense for that matter" (Doman, Doman, and Aisen, 1985, p. 18).

Contrast this approach with the stage theorists who argue that intelligence proceeds in a stagelike progression and that children cannot assimilate knowledge or solve problems that are inappropriate for the particular stage that they have reached. This means that the child's stage of cognitive development has to be identified and the curriculum calibrated accordingly (Copple, Sigel, and Saunders, 1984; Montessori, 1970). Thus, these two approaches to the trajectory of development agree that early experience has important long-term effects, but it is at that point that their commonality ends.

Beliefs as the Underpinnings of Preschool Programming. How have two such different approaches to early education developed and persisted? I argue that it is because of differences in *beliefs* about the nature of development and about ways to influence it. Beliefs, values, and attitudes about what children need have formed the basis for a great diversity of preschool programs, not just those described above. Preschool programs existed long before any formal, systematic program "models" had been developed (Osborn, 1980). In fact, it is safe to say that most preschool educational programs grew out of shrewd observations of children's needs, interests, and readiness to participate in a group experience, with those observations shaped by the observer's beliefs about what is important for children to know and to do (Biber, 1984; Montessori, 1970; Osborn, 1980).

Target Populations and Critical Experiences

We have seen that the trajectory principle is deeply ingrained in the belief system of parents and educators. We have also seen that its specific interpretation is related to the conceptual frameworks, developmental theories, and values that they espouse. Differences in these areas lead to disagreements about the kinds of early experiences that are critical in influencing the trajectory, and about how those experiences should be presented to the child. As the chapters in this volume illustrate, these questions cannot be debated meaningfully without considering the target populations to be served. Middle-class parents, for example, may have different values and beliefs about development than do less affluent parents, and programs for their children may have to meet different needs. Full-time working parents may think about early education differently than parents who do not have urgent child care requirements. Cultural and ethnic traditions also influence values and beliefs about the nature of early education and the kinds of developmental domains that need to be shaped in preschool education.

Social Class and Preschool Education. The chapters in this volume describe research and program models for two constituencies: the privileged, or children from middle- and upper-middle class families who can afford to send them to private preschools (studies by Hirsh-Pasek, Rescorla, and Hyson and some of Stipek's sample), and the underprivileged (Weikart and Schweinhart; Farran, Silveri, and Culp; and, to some extent, Zigler and Gilman).

Both poor and middle-class parents implicitly espouse the trajectory principle, but they may have different expectations about what aspects of development and behavior should be influenced by preschool experiences. Middle-class parents have often believed that children profit from preschool attendance because of its social nature. For example, in a recent study of preschool in three cultures, Tobin, Wu, and Davidson (1989) report results of interviews with 210 American parents who were asked, "Why should a society have preschool?" American parents (apparently middle class, although the authors do not give much detail about their sample) responded as follows: to give children a good start academically (22 percent), to give children experience at being a member of a group (20 percent), and to make young children more independent and self-reliant (23 percent).

In contrast, in an informal survey I did with poverty-level black parents whose children were enrolled in an early childhood program, parents reported that their primary goals were for the children to learn to behave, to do what they were told, and to stay out of trouble. If the children acquired these behaviors, the parents believed, they would get along in school and learn.

In addition to differences in parents' goals, program developers' rationales for preschools serving low-income and higher-income children have also differed. In the 1960s, belief in the trajectory principle led to the advocacy of preschool as an intervention effort to remedy the negative effects of poverty. Head Start epitomizes this effort. With massive support, Head Start was established as a solution to problems of poverty, school dropouts, poor health, delinquency, and family dysfunction. Recently, the public schools have become the setting for some of these intervention efforts. Although Zigler and Gilman regard public schools as potential sources of support for children and families, Farran, Silveri, and Culp raise some issues to consider when we locate preschool programs in these settings.

The rationale for developing preschool programs for privileged children has had a different tradition, which is also consistent with the trajectory principle. Historically, preschool attendance for middle-class children was justified as a way to enhance children's day-to-day social experiences by allowing them to engage with peers in a rich setting, and, in the longer run, to enhance their long-term socioemotional growth.

These contrasting rationales for preschool for low- and middle-class children may be converging, however. As the efficacy of cognitive programs for poor children became recognized, middle-class families became more interested in preschools that also stressed cognitive skills and academic achievement. Stipek's report and those by Rescorla, Hyson, and Hirsh-

Pasek offer some evidence of a strong emphasis on academic orientations for middle-class as well as low-income children, representing a shift away from the traditional child development approach. We may also speculate that parents' concern for young children's school achievement may be related to well-publicized comparisons of American children's performance in math and science with the performance of children from other countries. Furthermore, these values may be endemic to our society, which sees education as a means of entering the competitive world rather than as a means of personal enhancement. Whatever the reasons, middle-class parents used to want preschool purely as a social experience for their children. Now they seem to want a head start to Harvard.

Work, Family, and Preschool Education. Another reason for advocating preschool is that it serves as a child care setting for working parents. Zigler and Gilman describe the child care crisis in America and propose using public school buildings as settings for comprehensive programs of child care. Parents who are looking for full-time child care (whatever their social class) may well have different priorities and expectations than those of parents who have the option of home care for their children. However, preschool as an educational enterprise is independent of parents' needs for child care. In a sense, issues of the goals and content of preschool education can get confounded by social concerns about child care.

Cultural Traditions and Preschool Education. Preschool education seems to be an almost universal institution in most developed countries. However, the goals and reasons for its existence reflect cultural differences. For example, for 61 percent of a sample of Japanese parents, the function of preschool was primarily to provide children with the opportunity to be in a group, whereas only 20 percent of American parents and 12 percent of Chinese parents saw this purpose as a major goal (Tobin, Wu, and Davidson, 1989).

In summary, the interest in preschool education today cuts across social class, work status, and cultural and ethnic background. However, as we have seen, these groups may have very different reasons for their interest in early educational experiences.

Impact of Preschool Experiences

The trajectory perspective implies an interest in the long-term outcomes of preschool experiences, as evidenced by writers' frequent use of terms such as "program effectiveness" and "longitudinal impact." Here again, we need to emphasize the specificity of effects related to the target populations and the domains of development to be studied. Most studies of the effects of preschool have focused on academic achievement, although chapters in this volume go beyond this outcome (Hirsh-Pasek; Weikart and Schweinhart; Zigler and Gilman).

Preschool Education and Outcomes for Low-Income Children. Low-income children do seem to profit from preschool intervention programs. A number of studies have reported that preschool education has a long-term effect on school achievement as late as the eighth grade (Miller and Bizzell, 1983; Powell, 1987). However, not all preschool programs have the same long-term outcomes. Miller and Bizzell (1983) demonstrate quite clearly that nondidactic programs—Montessori and traditional child development preschools—have been the most effective. They report that although IQ scores did not differ among children when initially enrolled in four different types of preschool programs (Montessori, traditional, Darcee, and Bereiter and Engelmann), by the eighth grade differences were found in math and reading achievement scores. However, these differences were specific to certain groups of children. Miller and Bizzell (1983, p. 727) write, "Males from the two nondidactic programs (traditional child development and Montessori) were significantly higher in achievement than males from the two didactic programs (Darcee and Bereiter and Engelmann). Montessori males were consistently the highest group." In contrast, females seemed to profit from the didactic programs, although not significantly.

Moving beyond academic achievement, Weikart and Schweinhart provide further evidence of the benefits of preschool for low-income children. They show that preschool experiences seem to reduce the probability of delinquency and unemployment in later years (Schweinhart, Weikart, and Larner, 1986). In this volume, they offer evidence that nondidactic preschool programs have a particular advantage because of their association with lower levels of social alienation and antisocial behavior in adolescence.

Outcomes of Preschool for Middle- and Upper-Middle-Class Children. Turning to the short- and long-term consequences of preschool experiences for privileged children, the story looks quite different. In this volume, Hirsh-Pasek reports equivocal outcomes for middle-class children who attend academically oriented preschools. She writes that highly academic preschools had no extended effect on academic skills such as knowledge of letters and numbers. The initial advantage of attendance at an academic preschool dissipates by the time the child is in kindergarten. Is it reasonable to expect that these middle-class children will profit academically from preschool? Chances are that by the time most middle-class children enter kindergarten they have already mastered some of the essentials of letter and number recognition, and they may even know how to read. Having a formal program of this type probably does little to provide substantive knowledge, but it does seem to generate some anxiety about achievement.

The evidence for longer-term effects from such programs is spotty. To my knowledge there are, unfortunately, no longitudinal studies that have evaluated the influence of different types of preschool education for the privileged, comparable to the study by Miller and Bizzell (1983) of low-income children. If in fact these middle-class preschool experiences produce differences, the differences might well be in the metacognitive areas. In a program I directed for four-year-old middle-class children, those in the experimental program, which emphasized reflective thinking and teachers' use of inquiry strategies (distancing), were more likely to solve conservation problems and to use more abstract language than were children in a traditional program (Sigel, 1979).

There may be other, long-term effects of acceleration for middle-class children. On the basis of what child development experts might predict, the effects could be more evident in social-emotional domains, for example, achievement anxiety (Elkind, 1987; Sigel, 1987a, 1987b), than in academic or cognitive areas. Evidence of long-term effects is anecdotal and retrospective, but the Hirsh-Pasek chapter in this volume provides some suggestive data from a short-term follow-up of middle-class children.

Evaluating the Evaluation Research. Research on the costs and benefits of different types of preschool programs is difficult to conduct and to interpret. There is evidence that some preschool programs for low-income children have long-term effects, that is, do influence the developmental trajectory. Thus, optimism concerning the long-term outcomes of preschool may be justifiable and is certainly commendable. However, research has tended to focus on molar outcomes, such as IQ or academic achievement, and has not related the outcomes to specifics of the program. What are the characteristics of programs that have had a long-term influence? What correlated life experiences keep children on the track toward positive developmental outcomes? To answer these questions, both for low-income and middle-class preschool programs, we need to direct our research beyond cognitive and academic outcomes in order to examine process variables and the motivational and social systems that may serve a supportive function during and after the child's attendance at preschool (an argument that Stipek, and Zigler and Gilman also make in their respective chapters). A particular program's effectiveness may stem from a general factor rather than from some specific procedure. As Stipek notes, having a warm, supportive teacher might yield positive outcomes regardless of the formal curriculum model.

Conclusions and Recommendations

The chapters in this volume, as well as other research discussed here, demonstrate that although there is general agreement about the importance of early educational experiences for later development, the field is still fraught with disagreement about goals, methods, and outcomes. The variety of preschool programs described here, including those that are didactic or academic, is likely to persist in the future. As such, the selection of specific program approaches, and of criteria for evaluating those approaches, should perhaps be based on the needs of the target populations. Because different populations have different educational needs in preschool, educational programs can be developed for each particular group. Therefore, programs should be not only developmentally appropriate but also appropriate to parents' goals and children's particular needs, a point that Farran, Silveri, and Culp's research supports. The evidence is clearest for the benefits of preschool education for low-income children (Weikart and Schweinhart). For poor children, an early start may be useful because opportunities to enhance competencies or remediate problems enable these children to begin elementary school at a level comparable to their more affluent peers.

Programs for the privileged child are more controversial. Research reported in this volume shows little if any academic gain from an early academic emphasis by middle-class parents or preschools. Evidence reported in this volume and elsewhere (Miller and Bizzell, 1983; Copple, Sigel, and Saunders, 1984; Schweinhart, Weikart, and Larner, 1986) suggests that didactic, teacher-directed preschool programs tend to have negative outcomes, especially in the social-emotional domains. Both Stipek and Hyson have found that teachers in didactic, formally academic programs are less warm and more controlling than are their colleagues in child-centered programs. It is notable that the reported negative effects of didactic preschool programs cut across social class and have been found both in the short term (Hirsh-Pasek) and after a longer period of time (Weikart and Schweinhart).

If these negative effects are valid findings, why have didactic programs persisted in early childhood education? As discussed earlier, decisions about program goals and methods are often grounded in attitudes and beliefs that may not be amenable to change even in the face of contrary data. Smith and Shepard (1988) have convincingly shown that, among kindergarten teachers, advocacy of specific programs is related to underlying belief systems. Furthermore, many researchers have vested interests in particular program models or approaches, or are attempting to provide justification for federal support for particular kinds of early interventions. For example, Weikart and his colleagues have a vested interest in the cognitively oriented curriculum and are committed to it (Schweinhart, Weikart, and Larner, 1986). Others are similarly invested in Montessori programs. I am committed to the Child-as-a-Thinker model (Copple, Sigel, and Saunders, 1984). It may be possible to be dispassionate only if one does not have a commitment to any one program (for example, Rescorla, Hyson, and Hirsh-Pasek in this volume; Miller and Bizzell, 1983). Even so, research findings will probably have little effect in changing the minds of those who "own" programs.

Finally, in assessing the impact of preschool experiences, we need to focus not just on the curriculum or activities but also on the pressure that adults can create by enrolling children in these various programs and by stressing high academic and performance expectations at an early age. Clinical psychologists and psychotherapists have expressed these concerns to a greater extent than have educators and researchers. If early academics reflect "pressure," it may be because children have become valuable in satisfying their parents' desires and not their own.

References

Bereiter, C., and Engelmann, S. *Teaching Disadvantaged Children in the Preschool*. Englewood Cliffs, N.J.: Prentice-Hall, 1966.

Biber, B. *Early Education and Psychological Development*. New Haven, Conn.: Yale University Press, 1984.

Copple, C., Sigel, I. E., and Saunders, R. *Educating the Young Thinker: Classroom Strategies for Cognitive Growth*. Hillsdale, N.J.: Erlbaum, 1984. (Originally published 1979.)

Doman, G. J., Doman, J., and Aisen, S. *How to Give Your Baby Encyclopedic Knowledge*. Garden City, N.Y.: Doubleday, 1985.

Elkind, D. *Miseducation: Preschoolers at Risk*. New York: Knopf, 1987.

Miller, L. B., and Bizzell, R. P. "Long-Term Effects of Four Preschool Programs: Sixth, Seventh, and Eighth Grades." *Child Development*, 1983, *54*, 727–741.

Miller, L. B., and Dyer, J. L. *Four Preschool Programs: Their Dimensions and Effects*. Monographs of the Society for Research in Child Development, vol. 40, no. 5–6 (serial no. 162). Chicago: University of Chicago Press, 1975.

Montessori, M. *The Child in the Family*. (N. R. Cirillo, trans.) New York: Avon, 1970. (Originally published 1956.)

Osborn, D. K. *Early Childhood Education in Historical Perspective*. Athens, Ga.: Education Associates, 1980.

Powell, D. R. "Comparing Curricula and Practices: The State of Research." In S. L. Kagan and E. F. Zigler (eds.), *Early Schooling: The National Debate*. New Haven, Conn.: Yale University Press, 1987.

Schweinhart, L. J., Weikart, D. P., and Larner, M. B. "Consequences of Three Preschool Curriculum Models Through Age 15." *Early Childhood Research Quarterly*, 1986, *1*, 15–45.

Shapiro, E., and Biber, B. "The Education of Young Children: A Developmental-Interaction Approach." *Teachers College Record*, 1972, *74*, 55–79.

Sigel, I. E. "On Becoming a Thinker: A Psychoeducational Model." *Educational Psychologist*, 1979, *14*, 70–78.

Sigel, I. E. "Does Hothousing Rob Children of Their Childhood?" *Early Childhood Research Quarterly*, 1987a, *2*, 211–225.

Sigel, I. E. "Early Childhood Education: Developmental Enhancement or Developmental Acceleration?" In S. L. Kagan and E. F. Zigler (eds.), *Early Schooling: The National Debate*. New Haven, Conn.: Yale University Press, 1987b.

Smith, M. L., and Shepard, L. A. "Kindergarten Readiness and Retention: A Qualitative Study of Teachers' Beliefs and Practices." *American Educational Research Journal*, 1988, *25*, 307–333.

Tobin, J. J., Wu, D.Y.H., and Davidson, D. H. *Preschool in Three Cultures: Japan, China, and the United States*. New Haven, Conn.: Yale University Press, 1989.

Irving E. Sigel is senior research scientist at the Educational Testing Service in Princeton, New Jersey.

INDEX

ORDERING INFORMATION

NEW DIRECTIONS FOR CHILD DEVELOPMENT is a series of paperback books that presents the latest research findings on all aspects of children's psychological development, including their cognitive, social, moral, and emotional growth. Books in the series are published quarterly in Fall, Winter, Spring, and Summer and are available for purchase by subscription as well as by single copy.

SUBSCRIPTIONS for 1991 cost $48.00 for individuals (a savings of 20 percent over single-copy prices) and $70.00 for institutions, agencies, and libraries. Please do not send institutional checks for personal subscriptions. Standing orders are accepted.

SINGLE COPIES cost $15.95 when payment accompanies order. (California, New Jersey, New York, and Washington, D.C., residents please include appropriate sales tax.) Billed orders will be charged postage and handling.

DISCOUNTS FOR QUANTITY ORDERS are available. Please write to the address below for information.

ALL ORDERS must include either the name of an individual or an official purchase order number. Please submit your order as follows:
    Subscriptions: specify series and year subscription is to begin
    Single copies: include individual title code (such as CD1)

MAIL ALL ORDERS TO:
    Jossey-Bass Inc., Publishers
    350 Sansome Street
    San Francisco, California 94104

FOR SALES OUTSIDE OF THE UNITED STATES CONTACT:
    Maxwell Macmillan International Publishing Group
    866 Third Avenue
    New York, New York 10022

OTHER TITLES AVAILABLE IN THE
NEW DIRECTIONS FOR CHILD DEVELOPMENT SERIES
William Damon, Editor-in-Chief